"It was a very good kind of match, and also very bad...."

"They were both of them beautiful. They were also, both of them, in a kind of exile, and sought to find a home, a country, in one another, and very nearly did, came as close as maybe it is possible to do, but they were each so deep in exile when they met—and how would they have known that?

"My father, so successful, full of energy, in command of things.

"My mother, so seemingly established—a title even, money somewhere in the background, big houses, gardens, furniture, wax for the furniture, polish for the silver, manners, style, and more than style or manners, a seeming feel for independence, for being a 'new woman.' But the house my mother grew up in was a dead house, and when my father, running out of success, and nerve, and stamina, and command, came finally to seek shelter in that house—it turned out to have no room, it was already sinking, sunk....

"But that was all for later, for much later. It was later that they found those things out, or didn't find them out, just lived them, lived under them. In the beginning, though, it must have been lovely, as it often is."

EXILES
was originally published by
Farrar, Straus & Giroux, Inc.

Michael J. Arlen

Exiles

PUBLISHED BY POCKET BOOKS NEW YORK

Parts of this book originally appeared in **The New Yorker**

EXILES

Farrar, Straus & Giroux edition published May, 1970
Pocket Book edition published March, 1971

This *Pocket Book* edition includes every word
contained in the original, higher-priced edition. It is printed
from brand-new plates made from completely reset, clear, easy-to-read
type. *Pocket Book* editions are published by Pocket Books, a division
of Simon & Schuster, Inc., 630 Fifth Avenue, New York, N.Y. 10020.
Trademarks registered in the United States and other countries.

Exiles

$\mathcal{H}$E USED TO JOKE ABOUT BEING frail and weak, about having had TB as a boy, and then something wrong with his back, and then a car accident (he had been walking across a street) in Los Angeles—but he so clearly didn't really think himself frail or weak, and when things started going wrong for him, going wrong in him I guess was more like it, he couldn't countenance it at all. The pain, yes, or things like that. Discomfort is what they call it. He could manage that all very damned well. But not the fact of things truly starting to go wrong.

It happened in the spring, I think. I remember the time vaguely, April. It must have been spring, but I was in the Army then and not paying much attention to seasons. Fort Dix. White board barracks.

All that dust, and boots beside the bed, and those baggy dusty fatigues. A weird soft life, soft amid the weapons, the rifles, the machinery, the sounds of tank battalions and howitzers on the distant ranges. It was a telegram—one of those long telegrams with some of the key words hashed up by the local teletypist. They called me out of formation one morning, into the orderly room—the soft-faced, big-bellied, indoors sergeants sitting around at their desks having coffee. Some corporal handed me this thing, and I opened it and read it standing there. It seemed to read so easily, I read it right through. YOUR FATHER GOING INTO HOSPITAL TODAY . . . SUSPECTED CANCER . . . EXELLENT DOCTOR . . . CHANCES ARE GOOD . . . WILL KEEP YOU ADVISED. And in a strange way I believed it, believed anyway the calm codelike positivism of the message. *Suspected . . . Excellent . . . Chances are good . . . Will keep you advised*. My mother had a way with telegrams. It was one of the sergeants who snapped me out of it. "What is it, kid? Your girl got pregnant?" No, I said, my father's going into the hospital for an operation; and then I told him some more, and then they all started wheeling into line, stirring things up, papers, forms, one of the roundest and most dough-faced of the sergeants tap-tap-tapping out an emergency pass on a tiny typewriter in the corner. It was very nice, one of those acts of complicity. I couldn't quite understand it at the time and felt apart from them—these strangers who were evidently expressing their own fears and worries. I was too cool for that sort of thing. I could take an emergency three-day-pass or leave it alone. But then I got into New York, and we were suddenly there, inside, in one of those blank, beige, tiled, airless hospital corridors, my mother and I, and I could understand quite a bit.

We walked up and down, walked up and down, and sat. My mother smoked. I told her about Fort Dix. Nurses passed, and all the doctors in the world. Finally, Doctor Gregson appeared—that was his name, Gregson. An excellent surgeon. One of the great surgeons. One of the really great, the very best. He was carrying a trim blue canvas case that unmistakably contained a tennis racket, and was buttoning up his jacket. He had just come from changing and was obviously in a hurry. "I think we got it all," he said to my mother. "It had spread quite far into the lymph. We had to take out a lung . . ." A few more sentences like that, and off he went. My father was never the same after Gregson, which is unfair to Gregson, since he doubtless would have died sooner, and probably worse, without him. Maybe if I hadn't met Gregson just then, and just that way, that busy on-my-way-to-the-River-Club look, that bloody tennis racket, like a figure out of some second-rate country-house comedy, I wouldn't still have such a particular sense of that moment in time, of an act ending that afternoon in the hospital. But it's true, he wasn't the same afterwards. There was something crucial gone from him, and not just the lung either, although that certainly didn't help; and neither did the information we received later that the removal of the lung had been more in the nature of a "hunch" than a step that had been absolutely necessary.

It was so terrible really. He knew the lung was gone, and hated that, one more infirmity, and tried to make jokes about it although the jokes wouldn't take. But he didn't really believe about the rest. He would just lie in bed, at first in bed at the hospital, and then in bed at home, and then sitting up at home, and wait for something to happen to him, something to come back to him. In appearance, it wasn't quite all that passive, and much of the time he seemed "fine." He had the wit and the irony and the strength or whatever it is that enables some people not to survive bad things but somehow to move with grace above them—he could do that part of it very well, and down to the moment he died, about one year later, he managed to "be himself," to be elegant, to be amusing, to be even gay. But there was something gone, and he was then only sixty, "only sixty," whatever that means, and sometimes a look would cross his face, and linger there for a second, and surprise even him, I think, with its weight and bitterness.

In Paris, I remember, about six months later, we met, the three of us, a ghastly meeting really, the weather gray and sour and full of wet, which sometimes doesn't matter too much but then it seemed as if the whole earth, all the grass and trees and leaves and everything bright and sunlit had disappeared, was disappearing, and for good and all. I'd gone over to Germany in the Army, and my mother and father had recently gone back to Europe on one of those trips that are supposed to give sick people a health-instilling change of air or scene—I don't know why hanging around hotels is supposed to be good for people who are feeling lousy, but it seems to be something that people who feel lousy find hard to resist. Anyway there they were, two weeks at the bright and tacky Dorchester in London, and then to the Lotti in Paris. I can't imagine why the Lotti, with its hush, and tiny shipboard corridors, and half-dead old ladies in the lobby—I think they probably felt that the gap between the way they were really feeling and the way the Ritz would expect, or would remind, them to feel would be too great. I came to see them there one weekend. They were in one of those small-windowed, thick-carpeted old rooms with lots of gilt and low-watt lightbulbs. The breakfast tray on the bed. A pile of books on a chair. Detective stories. *The Devils of Loudun.* The picture my mother always traveled with (a small blue watercolor of a Mediterranean scene, an island) on the bedside table. The curtains drawn. They both were very quiet.

My mother's sister was then in Paris, and so was one of my mother's few old close friends, Louise Ferande—Madame Ferande, who did something at one of the couture houses, a tiny bony woman with one of those sharp, animated, uninterested faces. That first evening we all had drinks together, the five of us perched around a table in the tiny Lotti bar, my aunt talking at length about her hardships, which was okay, since she led, more or less by intent, a life so full of human drama and collision that, like a racing-car driver, she seemed to exist most naturally midpoint between some past near-miss and some awaited one. Right then she was having trouble with her lawyer, who was trying to cheat her, so she said. We talked about that for a while. My father didn't talk much at all. These women could be such bitches really, and then when he had left the bar for a moment they all crowded over the table and cooed and trilled about how marvelous he was, in such good shape, so elegant, not thin at all, well maybe a few pounds, but not *thin,* such good *color.* He was nearly dead by then, I think my mother knew that. I think he was beginning to know that. And then the next day it almost happened. In the morning, at dawn, he had some sort of seizure, something to do with the heart, the heart maybe working too hard because of there being only one lung. I don't know, it doesn't matter. But off he was taken suddenly, a now-strange city, a strange hotel, a strange doctor, a strange hospital, some small place out near Neuilly. He was okay, they said out there. The doctor was okay too. Nice. Sympathetic. But Christ how crummy it all was— wet, gray, faraway; and he lying there in the bed, he seemed so small, and getting smaller. I would go out there with my mother, or sometimes alone, and sit beside the bed, the French nurses running in and out, and try to tell him things about my life, what-I-was-doing, because that seemed to please him. What I was doing. Nothing. I was in the Army. He had this funny idea, I remember, about the Army, about me and the Army, and he hated for me to tell him that I thought it all a lot of nonsense, or especially that I was messing around with it at all. Sometimes, in order to liven things up, I would tell him of some small adventure, an overstayed pass, a wangled assignment—and he really wouldn't have any of it. He wanted me to be a good boy in the Army. The sheet that covered him up to the neck, I remember, rose and fell with the slow rhythm of his breathing. The sound of his breathing filled the room. I talked informatively of the military life.

He got better for a while. The heart was okay, they said, but naturally one must take it easy. He left the little hospital in Neuilly. He was so pleased his heart was okay. He would take brief walks outside the Lotti in the pale sidewalk sun, and have a gin with Joe Baldwin at the Travellers, and get absurdly, miserably, tired. But he was somehow pleased, maybe at just being alive. And then, around the middle of May, they went on down to the South of France. It was a good time for them, I think. They stayed at the Carlton, the big white dumpy Carlton, with the two domed towers, and the dingy little beach, and the bar, the great Carlton bar, where everyone had once sat around, where everyone had once waited for everyone else. Now everyone gone, or nearly, or just not around, or no longer interested. A p.r. man from M.G.M. where Willie Maugham once sat. Two dozen outboards rocketing and churning up the Mediterranean. But still the Mediterranean. In late May my sister went down there for a while. He seems much better, my sister wrote me, hoping it was true. My sister was then attempting to recover from a disastrous romance with an Egyptian (to whom she had been introduced by my aunt), and had taken briefly to writing me letters. My mother also wrote me letters. They were having a nice time. They took walks. They had seen such-and-such. My sister was still being very silly about Ari, who clearly had no visible means of support, and was a bounder, and so forth. Once, on a mostly spurious assignment for the Army newspaper, I ended up one May afternoon in North Africa, covering a golf match at a Moroccan air base, and phoned my parents, full of my new role as foreign correspondent (a military-golfing foreign correspondent), to announce that I might just "drop by" through Nice, where I knew the Air Force ran another flight. But they were having none of that. "That certainly doesn't sound sensible to me," my mother said, which in her language was the equivalent of cursing solidly for twenty minutes. My father naturally didn't want to hear about any of it. If the Army says you should be in Germany, he said, you should be in Germany. But they were well, or sounded well, and that really was good to hear. In a number of ways it must have been horrid then in Cannes, but they had managed a nice time, and that says something about something. I think it was probably the last nice time like that either of them had.

They came on home to New York later that summer, and my father thought he was actually on-the-mend, getting better, feeling better all the time, longer lunches, longer walks, improvement, health, perfection, life, everything better. But then it wasn't so at all. It wasn't better. It was worse. It was awful, that—he couldn't understand it. He was suddenly so tired, couldn't do anything. He felt very bad one day on his way out to lunch, very very bad, and went to bed. He postponed the lunch, which was with a man from *Time* who was researching a piece on Aldous Huxley, postponed it until the next week, but he never went out again. It was clear then that the doctors hadn't chopped it all out after all; that the excellent bright-eyed tennis-playing surgeon hadn't quite "caught it all," whatever "it" means in these instances. Cancer. The black dank specter. The fifth horseman. He so clearly had it, and even then would not quite believe it. Certainly no one told him that he must believe it, why should anyone tell a man that? He was indoors all the time then. Upstairs in bed for most of the day, and then sometimes, later in the afternoon, downstairs in the library. I had since come back from Europe, back from the Army to my job at Time-Life, and in a fit of filial affection (I think it was that) had set aside my plans for getting-my-own-place—girls, wild parties, at least the pleasures of leaving one's dirty laundry in the middle of the floor—and had moved back into my old room in their apartment. There was such death in that place. In a way, it had always had something of that feeling—an indoors, inward-facing apartment to begin with, short on sunlight, and heavy with my mother's tastes in embroidery, tapestry, thick fabrics, dark wood, dark things, closed curtains, little froufrous here and there for "gaiety" which only made it all worse. And now there was real death. Sometimes you could almost see it moving into him, the thin edge of a tide moving across the open water. He was so bright, he was still so bright. Mostly he read all the time now, or slept (or slept while reading), and sometimes talked a little with a faint, troubled, hard-of-breathing voice. But sometimes he would connect with something, a memory, an object moving far off across the horizon, and for a few moments would come awake, really awake, the eyes alive, that marvelous quickness, lightness, that so un-Anglo-Saxon passion pushing its way back into his voice, taking him with it, taking him now in some pain, in some considerable pain because of it, even laughing, his breath very short, his eyes seeming to see *out* for the first time in days or weeks; and then suddenly over, the sentence finished, the eyes dull, the breath coming in great gulps, while we sat around him feeling love and fear, fear for all of us. Death is a hard person to have in the house with one, and I don't know that I was too much help. I couldn't bear the smell of death, couldn't in fact bear to be there, was always finding reasons to get out, and later feeling terrible for having done so. Swearing I would act better. Would not duck out after dinner like that again. For whole days, maybe two days, would sit there dutiful, attentive, providing little bits of talk and whatever affection seemed transmittable —until one evening there I would be again. I'm sorry. I forgot. Have to meet. Won't be long. Won't be late. Didn't think you'd mind, yes, have a good night. See-you-in-the-morning.

He died in June, the last week in June. It was one of those steamy New York summers, everything

17

unnaturally hot, the air heavy, dusty. I'd just come back from an assignment up around Boston and was downtown at the office typing up notes. My sister called me there in the afternoon. He'd gotten very bad, she said, the doctor was there. I went on home. The doctor was leaving when I arrived. He said he was okay, which seemed an odd thing to say about a man with obviously terminal cancer, but he meant he was okay for then. Okay, considering. I went up to see him, but there was a new nurse. He's resting, she said. I went back down the stairs. My mother came down presently. He had this pressure on the lung, she said, almost instructively, and went on to tell me the details of where the pressure came from, what had happened, what the lung could take and so forth. She lived in the details, they supported her. How is he now? I asked. He seems back to normal, she said. It all seemed crazy, and I knew that he would die tomorrow, or that night, or the next day. The next morning he was awake and I went in to see him. He was pretty tired, but smiled, and we exchanged a few words. I told him a little about the Boston trip. "It's important you go to the office," my mother said. "It's important things go on as normal." I went down to the office, towards the office, getting as far as Sixtieth Street, and then came on back. My mother was angry but it didn't matter too much. I stayed in my room reading, or doing nothing, and then around lunchtime I went in again to see him.

It was around twelve o'clock, about the only time of day that room ever got any sunlight. He was sitting up in the big bed, with a tray, but not very mindful of the tray. Such a small fierce man. He seemed extraordinarily alive just then, his eyes a deep deep brown and full of life and warmth. We talked, or rather, for the first time it seemed in weeks, in months, he talked. Not very much. About books, as I remember. Some book of Arnold Bennett's that he'd been re-reading, or trying to: *Riceyman Steps.* "I know you don't read Bennett now," he said, "but you ought to look at him. He wrote some good books." And: "It's funny, isn't it, when I was your age, Bennett was one of my Field Marshalls. I was a corporal, and Wells and Bennett were my Field Marshalls." And: "Bennett and I had lunch together once. I can't remember why. At the Savoy. Bennett talked the whole time about money." He smiled. He seemed very happy. Charles Hughson, a friend of his from England, was in town, and I mentioned that to him, and he talked a little about when they'd first met—Hughson a young reader or some such at Victor Gollancz, and he then new to London, new to writing, new to everything, a young man in a small room off Shepherds Market. His breath seemed almost steady then. He held my hand for a moment. His eyes were half closed as he talked, the man in the bed in New York talking across the years to the man in the small room in

19

Shepherds Market. And then he said he was tired. I think I'll just sleep for a while is what he said. And I took his tray up, which had a thing of custard on it that he hadn't touched, and carried it down. And twenty minutes later, the nurse, who had looked in on him, came down the stairs to tell us he was dead.

$\mathcal{A}$N OLD BROWN-TINTED PHOTOGRAPH mounted on thick cardboard. A round-faced, plain, American-looking girl, but with fine eyes; fine, wide, brave, open eyes. At least, that is the way she seems in the photograph. A long time back. New York. The date, 1881, which was the year, I just remember, that Henry James (who signed himself then Henry James, Jr.) first published *The Portrait of a Lady*— not that they ever met, had tea (which later wouldn't have been all that unlikely), or had any kind of actual connection with each other, but I suppose I make some kind of connection between them in my own mind. Two émigrés.

Her name was Abby Wright. Abigail Pankhurst Wright of Cleveland. The youngest of several children of a Cleveland businessman. A small business-man. I don't know anything about the rest of her family, about her parents. She had red hair, and was short in height, even for then, about five feet or so, not more, and was said to have a magnificent temper; and she was my great-grandmother, my mother's grandmother. Only by the time I knew her she was no longer Abby Wright of Cleveland, looking as proud and scared as a serving girl in the unfamiliar studio of an unfamiliar New York photographer; she was somebody, or something, called Madame la Princesse Daria Kara-Georgevitch, and she lived in a huge house down the hill from us in Cannes, the Villa Fiorentina, with its endless terraces of Italian-ate gardens (box hedges garishly trimmed into shapes of animals, birds, whatnot), footmen, camellias, a lovely chapel right beside the house that members of the family used every five years or so for wed-dings, and that I used in between times to hide in and make great resonant, wheezing sounds upon the foot-pedal organ in the upstairs loft.

When I look at that early photograph, the one from 1881 of the young girl with the round plain face, it's so hard to try to even imagine what it all must have been like then. She'd married early, at seventeen or eighteen—a man called Edward Wright, also young, a young man of ambition who had started a steamship company on the Great Lakes, the Garland Steamship Company of Chicago, and had done that for a few years; and then shortly after their first child was born he had decided apparently to get away from Chicago, which was where they were living, to get out of the Midwest, and steamships, to do something more adventurous. And so he had gone out to Montana—there was talk of mining and mineral rights and great finds in the earth. It must have been an adventurous time then, and so he went out that year, and he was killed. Nobody ever seemed to know why or how, but he was killed. I think I was once told "by Indians," which certainly might have been true, but my guess is that I made that part of it up. In those days it could have been by any number of ways, and the more I think of the very little I know about him, the more I think it is probably truer to just leave it the way they all had left it at the time—he died somewhere in Montana, somehow, in 1880. And a year later, his young wife, very young, with a small baby, faced, one guesses, with the prospect of living out her days in Cleveland or Chicago, under the umbrella of various parents and relatives—well, she clearly had her own ambitions and she got the hell out.

And went to Europe. The two of them. London first; then "the Continent." It must have been very strange, although she had some money then, which doubtless helped. The Garland Steamship Company had made some money, and in due course she sold her shares in that and let the bank in Cleveland handle the rest. She had, I guess, plenty to live on in a modest sort of way, modest hotels, modest "resorts," and so that is what they did, my great-grandmother and the small girl who was my grandmother, they toured, they traveled around Europe. Steamer trunks on railway platforms. Porters. Luggage. Aix-les-Bains. "The mountains." Paris. London. "The seashore." And periodically they would come back to Cleveland—endless three-week voyages on cumbersome, rolling, sailing-steamers, deck chairs, winds, spilled food; I remember my grandmother once telling me how terrified she used to be of "the crossing," although I'm afraid that part of her inheritance from those hotel years turned out to be that she became terrified of nearly everything. She married young, too —my grandmother. She always seemed to me a sad, strange, lonely woman—pretty in that depressing fragile way, which was maybe more the fashion then, although I doubt that it was ever the fashion. All those years *en route*. Governesses teaching one French verbs in small hotel rooms. She married at eighteen—my mother's father. Alexandre Mercati. Count Alexandre Mercati, a young Greek on the rise in "court circles" in Athens. They met one winter in Saint-Moritz—there is a lovely picture of him then. Tall, dark, a bristling mustache, stiff collar, hair plastered down. A real Count right out of a Phillips Oppenheim novel, which he really wasn't like at all.

24

(Privately, anyway; he liked to farm.) But looking at the photograph, and remembering my grandmother, who seemed so frail and fragile and falling-down at forty-five (one could imagine her in a perpetual swoon of vapors all her girlhood), it's not hard to conceive of the attraction between her and this stern, dark, impassive man. They were married at any rate, and lived in Athens, lived for a half dozen years in Athens, where my uncle, mother, and then my aunt were born (three children with neo-classical names: Leonardo, Atalanta, Daria); and he, Alexandre, attended well to his duties—attended to the King of Greece, did God knows what, was sort of an arranger, an aide, a staff man, became something called Chamberlain, Lord Chamberlain. I remember one summer we were in Athens, long ago—he came by our hotel room with his court uniform on (it was the first time I had seen it), a splendiferous thing with braid and silk, and knee breeches, and lots of medals. There was a small revolutionary scuffle going on in the streets that day. Anarchists. Socialists. Some rifle fire across the square. He took the medals off in our hotel room, I remember, and put them very carefully in a case, a blue velvet case, and hurried out again. He was quite beautiful. He visited us a few times in the South of France. A tall, grave man. Gray-haired. A great gray mustache. On sunny days he'd get up very early in the morning, long before anyone else, and sit outside on the veranda

25

steps polishing his boots, and sometimes take revolver practice across the empty lawns. He was a very nice man, I always thought, although I don't know that we exchanged two words.

A few months after the birth of their youngest child (my aunt), his wife left him to run off with "another man," another strong, stony young man on the rise in diplomatic circles, an Austrian called Emerich von Pflugl (Baron Emerich von Pflugl in point of fact), not exactly a mellifluous sort of a name, and not exactly a very mellifluous sort of a person. Imre we called him. Uncle Imre—none of this step-grandfather business, which is what he became. I don't know how it all came about, how does anyone else know these things? The usual reasons probably, abetted by the fact that my grandmother felt herself congenitally hard-done-by and full of unattended-to sensibilities (and disliked Athens), that my grandfather was doubtless more than usually aloof and impassive even for those days, and that Imre (I don't think I'm really being unfair here) knew a good deal when he saw one. There are some letters remaining from that period, in a way terrifyingly inhuman letters despite the heat of rhetoric, full mostly of the sounds of social embarrassment and a kind of detached outrage. How could she & so forth. How could you. Think of my position. Think of *my* position . . . It must have been awful, though, awful all the way around, and especially for

Mercati because he really was a warm familial man, although he mightn't have been too adept at being so for her. Imre, Lord knows, didn't seem any better. He was okay in a way, but so damned Teutonic. Prussian. He even looked a bit like Erich von Stroheim, at least when I knew him. Round, bald, bullet-head, and, yes, one of those eye patches—he'd been wounded in the First World War, in the Austro-Hungarian cavalry—and long after my grandmother died he lived out his days, which is just exactly the way it was, in the Hotel Continental in Cambridge, Mass., in a tiny room (I was in college nearby and would have stiff lunches with him once or twice a year; which seemed enough for both of us), compiling some sort of Philosophy of Militarism.

But my grandfather, Mercati—well, he was left the children, including this young baby, while his wife was scooting off and away on the high seas back to America. And then, soon afterwards, his own life started to really fall apart, in the sense that he was simply and definitely on the wrong side of the great social upheavals that were beginning to take place all over Europe. In Greece, there was a revolution led by the socialist Sophocles Venizelos (evidently a remarkable man; great shock of hair, blazing eyes) and the King was tossed out. Everyone connected to the King was tossed out, and those especially connected to the King were shot. My grandfather was taken to be shot, but wasn't, because—I later found out

27

(found out from various sources, one of which, in
those nearly predictable ironies of history, turned out
to be Venizelos's chic granddaughter, whom I found
myself taking to fox-trotty little New York dances
some thirty-five years later)—because apparently
even Venizelos thought he was a nice man (I guess
the translation for that is "harmless") and because
he had all these damned children on his hands. He,
and they, were sent into exile instead, on the island
of Zante, which is one of the islands up there on
the northwest coast of Greece, some hundred miles
due south of Corfu. And stayed there for about ten
years. My uncle and mother and aunt more or less
grew up on Zante, a small house on a barren lovely
island, not entirely barren—donkeys, goats, shepherds, small villages, farms, olive trees. Mercati's
sister, Cecile, took care of the household. French
ladies would arrive every so often to teach the
children arithmetic and verbs. My uncle and my mother tried to keep scorpions as pets. Mercati wrote in
his journal. And then eventually a counterrevolution
took place, and brought them all back again—to
schools, and proper clothes, and big houses, and
"mountains" and "seashores" and Saint-Moritz in the
winter, and a curtsy to the King at birthday parties,
and yes, Balliol for my uncle, and finishing schools
in Paris, and God knows what else, what all, except
that when my mother peered back through her life,
back through her marriage, before her marriage, one

sensed that all she ever seemed to see that made any
sense to her was the dust of Zante, the donkeys and
scorpions, a passing remembrance, for instance, of
her father one afternoon standing solitary by the sea;
and that, in the strange ways of the world, everything
thereafter had been a kind of exile.

Marriage, even. Or especially. It's indeed hard
to know these things. When my mother and father
married—in many ways they were very old-fashioned; and in many ways they were some of the first
"modern" people, not so much in that my mother
smoked cigarettes in public, or that my father would
rather fly the Channel than take the boat across, but
in that the possibilities they, and people like them,
were beginning to live with were already then, dimly,
unknowingly, beginning to outrun their resources.
Possibilities everywhere. The ability to move. To
seize new ground. New people. New money. One
still had the old, of course. The old everything.
(Franz-Josef himself was not so many years dead.)
Then, one still had the old, the carpet underfoot,
the furniture nailed in place, although one was moving away from that with every breath, every year.
My father and mother met, as it happens, in Saint-
Moritz, and fell in love. My father would have been
then twenty-nine, and already "successful," a celebrity of some sort, but definitely not the right sort—
a novelist, a foreigner, really the most unbecoming
kind of foreigner. They fell very much in love that

29

winter, and then spent an anguished year alternately
together, apart, together, apart—her father disapproved. An adventurer is what he said he was. "No
better than an adventurer." I have one of the letters.
It is hard to realize that people once actually spoke
like that outside of novels, but then they often don't
speak all that differently now. They decided to get
married anyway, she running off towards the South
of France, to Cannes, to where my great-grandmother lived. Her father, the Count, sent quiversful of
letters in pursuit. Telegrams, those portentous, expensive telegrams of the early days of "wireless." He
disinherited her by telegram—it sounds so funny
now. Disinherit? We are above all that. But it must
have been bloody awful at the time (the man on
the beach at Zante); rejection in any form is bloody
awful.

In the end, though, it was okay, as these things
often seem to be if you have the nerve for them. A
big wedding. (They used the chapel once again.)
Marriage. Even Mercati relented a few years later,
and re-inherited her, or whatever, with some real
estate outside of Athens, which the next government
promptly impounded. It was a very good kind of
match, and also very bad, although I grant that it is
difficult to tell about these things by looking in from
outside the window. They were both of them beautiful. They were also, both of them, in a kind of

exile, and sought to find a home, a country, in one another, and very nearly did, came as close as maybe it is possible to do, but they were each so deep in exile when they met—and how would they have known that? My father, so successful, full of energy, in command of things. My mother, so seemingly established—a title even, money somewhere in the background, big houses, gardens, furniture, wax for the furniture, polish for the silver, manners, style, and more than style or manners, a seeming feel for independence, for being a "new woman." But the house my mother grew up in was a dead house, and when my father, running out of success, and nerve, and stamina, and command, came finally to seek shelter in that house—it turned out to have no room, it was already sinking, sunk. And my mother, seeking to escape from her (still unknown) exile, from all those mannered, fragile, assured, protected, self-protective people into this unusual man's vitality, life, imagination, energy—well, as maybe with many men, it turned out to be a fragile, an especially fragile kind of energy. So delicate, really. Too delicate. But that was all for later, for much later. It was later that they found those things out, or didn't find them out, just lived them, lived under them. In the beginning, though, it must have been lovely, as it often is. There is a picture of the two of them on a rock near Cannes, a picture of two bodies really, pleased with each other. I mean, there are clothes, and they

are looking in different directions, and there is even
someone else in the picture, a friend, but the picture is of what I said it was, and life must surely
have been like that for a while. The South of France.
The early 1930's. A white house on the side of a hill
above Cannes, wisteria, magnolia, lemon trees, fig
trees, green lawns, bamboo—about a half mile or so
above my great-grandmother's house. Madame la
Princesse—about ten years previously she had finally
remarried, at fifty-five, to somebody called Alexis
Kara-Georgevitch (M. le Prince), a nice man I
gather, one of the thousands of Kara-Georgevitches
unleashed upon an unprepared world after the
disappearance of Serbia, who then died a few years
later in a seaplane crash. One of the *first* seaplanes,
she used to say with genuine pride. She considered
herself a true modernist, or tried hard to be. I
remember this machine she had downstairs in her
salon, a room full of marble and porcelain and velvet,
immense Chinese screens, a harp over by the window—and there off to one side, built into the wall,
one of the first automatic record-changers, a marvelous untamed contraption consisting of a gramophone
turntable and a sort of obscene metallic hand, a
hand, that whirred and clanked and extended slowly
out of the wall, and grabbed the record, and then
usually dashed it to bits against the floor. I used to
go there sometimes for lunch. The two of us (only
one footman). Lamb chops. Mint sauce, the smell

of mint everywhere. Sunlight. She had very white hair then, and a kind, no-nonsense smile. I don't remember what we talked about. And afterwards we'd sit for a while outside, and she would read, and fall asleep, and I'd throw gravel at the peacocks.

I HAVE AN IDEA, NOW, FINALLY, OF what my father was like when I last saw him. Of what he looked like. Of what he sounded like. Even (I count myself lucky for this) a small idea of the kind of man he was. I have a picture anyway of him and me in the last couple of years before he died, a picture in which we are both fairly clear, are clear to each other, seem to touch. But all those years before. There are few pictures, and the ones that still remain seem now so very blurred. I've wondered how clear they were to him.

THERE WAS THAT TIME in California. Right after D-day, I remember. I was at school in New Hampshire.

St. Paul's, that fine, sleek, red-bricked, well-mowed, well-scrubbed Episcopal school that my mother had finagled me into just before the start of the school year. At least that was her story and I had no reason to doubt it. "Freddy Boissevain has been such a help," she said to me later. "You are lucky to have him on your side." Freddy Boissevain was apparently the man who had done the finagling. Freddy Boissevain was a trustee of the school, a tiny pink man with a soft face who would now and then drop by my mother's small apartment in New York and talk to her about electric utilities. He was a "fixer," my mother would say of him admiringly—he fixed people into weddings, and into clubs, and through customs, and into hotels, and maybe in and out of electric utilities on the side, and now he had fixed me into this fine sleek Episcopal school. I was terrified by it. I loved it. All those hymns. They were the same hymns I had been mumbling through at English schools and Canadian schools since the age of eight, and now I knew them nearly all by heart, I could yell them almost, and sometimes did when the music was loud enough, standing blazered and half asleep in chapel every morning beside the sturdy blond Protestant figures of the sons of stockbrokers and lawyers in the pews beside me. My mother kept telling me I should feel lucky to be there. I did feel lucky to be there. Showers that ran in never-ending streams of hot water. Food of such extraordinary delicacy that it could frequently be eaten without catchup. Teachers, even, who seemed to have taken up their calling with at least a semblance of vocation —at any rate unlike my previous masters, who had generally given such evidence of despising both the school and their profession that one assumed they had been sent to it, like us, for some sort of as-yet-unrevealed misdemeanor. It was a nice place, that school in New Hampshire. Lots of trees, and grass, and woods, and ponds. I had two friends there that first fall, Dick Hobart and George Brock (I don't remember why they were good friends, but they were), and we used to skip football practice some afternoons and go roaming through the woods in the back of the playing fields, nothing very poetic about it, we were looking for a supposed secret way into a nearby village, and eventually found it; but it was nice crashing about in the woods, even when it got cold, towards November. Even when the sun went down very early, and the trees were bare, and the ground hard, and everything in the world seemed brittle, except us, I think. And then my mother phoned me one evening. It was a big deal then, being phoned by one's mother. Messages were taken, transmitted, passed up channels, down channels. One was summoned to the housemaster's office. One was given slips of paper. Fear. Excitement. One called New York . . . New York City. The Butterfield number. "It's me," I said. "Well of course," she

said. And then: "He's coming over. He left a week
ago. I just got the cable." My father was finally
coming over from England, in some Brazilian freighter or something, bound for Halifax, Boston, New
York, the long way around. She was quite wild at
first, I couldn't make her out. I didn't feel much of
anything myself, except her wildness, her excitement.
I hadn't seen my father for nearly four years, and
when she'd say "your father" this, "your father" that,
I really had no face at all to connect the name to,
just a sort of shape, a feeling. An overcoat, in truth,
was what I most had to connect with in my mind—
there was this overcoat, this arm stretching from a
dark overcoat that pulled me, tugged me, laughing,
running, down a street off Berkeley Square. But anyway I was to come on down for his arrival. It had
been arranged with the school. A certain weekend.
Travel arrangements were being made; were made.
One week later I went on down. Concord to Boston.
Boston to New York. The junior master who put me
on the train at the Concord station kept tying tags
to my lapel, and I kept tearing them off—there
ought, I felt, to have been some benefit accrued by
then from all those past train journeys, at least to the
extent of not having to wear some damned tag on
one's lapel. "Don't forget you change stations in Boston," he said. He was a nice young man called Mr.
Stevens, who taught French, and had been on the
crew at Yale. "I know," I said. "South Station," he

said. "You change from North Station to South Station," he said. "I know," I said. The train chugged in, I stepped aboard. "Have a great time with your dad," said Mr. Stevens. "Here," he said, "take this—" and handed me the newspaper he had under his arm. I went down to New York but my father was not due in for still another week. My mother had just found out that morning, a cable from the ship—there had been some sort of trouble in a storm, they were bypassing Halifax, their speed had been reduced . . . My mother was too distracted by it all to give much thought to whether or not I was disappointed, which I wasn't. Something was supposed to have happened which apparently wasn't going to happen, at least not on schedule. But it was all too remote for disappointment. She wasn't disappointed in that sense either—just in limbo, not there. Not here. Not there. We went out to lunch that Saturday, I remember, and she asked me vaguely about school, and offered to go to a movie afterwards, but neither of us could think of one, neither of us much wanted to sit inside a movie house, she clearly couldn't sit still anywhere. I went on back to school, and then, indeed, about a week later my father phoned from New York, from that apartment. I spoke to him on the telephone. I had never heard his voice before, had quite forgotten it—and he then had all this feeling in it; he kept reaching out, and I knew it, felt all sorts of strange and powerful things myself.

But I had never heard his voice before. "How are you?" he kept saying helplessly, and I, equally help-less, would answer "Fine," or something like that. It must have been very hard for him. So many things must have been hard for him then, only the least of them being a three-and-a-half-week North Atlantic crossing on a glued-together Brazilian freighter. He was forty-eight years old. He had wanted to be so good, so shining, so flashing, such a proud exotic animal—he had had all these things, nearly had them, had his hands around them, had fondled them. The books. Money. The sun shining on silver. Flame. All those bright bright whites and blues beside the Mediterranean. The big silent cars. The speedboats. The drive along the Corniche and over the hills to Monte Carlo. Byzantium. At Maxine Elliott's, he and Willie Maugham would lunch (se-rene amid all those monkeys and the half-mad wild deer she kept about her); and Vincent Sheean; and Freddy Lewisohn; and sometimes Churchill would come by, Winston, who was writing all those pieces for *Collier's,* and talked, and drank, and sometimes went off to paint in the afternoons. And then it had all begun to go. The sun on the white houses. The sun on the Mediterranean. The sun on everything. Even as a kid I can remember it changing—a whole new sequence of snapshots. My father listening each evening to the B.B.C.'s Empire Service. Fouchard, the old gardener, absently oiling his 1918 rifle. The

39

evil-looking, brown-tinted drawings about gas masks and tanks and barrage balloons that started appearing in *The Illustrated London News*. It is easy enough, I guess, to look back with hindsight and talk smoothly about "Europe dancing" while the "storm clouds gathered," and I suppose there was some of that going on, I suppose there always is. But the people I peer back towards—I don't know that in the end they will turn out to have acted much differently towards their time than you or me; which is to say that when the dark shapes finally rose above the horizon, finally appeared, inescapably visible, above the horizon line, they worried, felt bad, were scared, were not scared, tried to do certain things knowing that the things they tried were only things, no more than things, and that by then, irreversibly, they were in the grip of "forces." My father, as I think of it, and people like him, lived his life in terms of a never-ending adjustment of his dream of it to what he saw was there to be adjusted to, lived with; and although I think it sad in many ways that this should be so, I'm not sure that many of us in any generation get much beyond that. It so happened (I believe) that his dream was shinier than most, full of wilder colors, plumage, smoke, honeysuckle, scents, the feel sometimes (it must have been) of perfect ivory; but then his view of what lay before his eyes at any given moment could also be colder, harder than most; full of less self-pity.

And so the world he had tried so hard to blow his shiny dream upon turned cold and sour, and he knew it, I think, as well as anyone; knew why; felt powerless to stop it, which is neither particularly to his credit nor his discredit. It is just the way things were for him. And then the war did come, arrived. We were in England. I had just gone off to school, my first school, a posh little cold-showers-and-Latin boarding school in Surrey. And we disbanded, our family, for "safety's" sake—I first, in a boatload of sniffly, properly capped-and-jacketed English boarding-school boys bound for another school in Canada. My mother and sister to New York. And he stayed there. In England. It was his adopted country, he used to say, conscious that people did not expect that sort of sentimentality from him, and conscious that he felt it, helplessly and absolutely. He was in London first, and then in Coventry, where he was what he could be, an air-raid warden—in actual title an "information officer" for Civil Defense, but mostly an air-raid warden—and felt proud of it. There was a lot of bombing there, in that war, in that place (as is remembered by some), and he did what he could, which was usually nothing, and felt scared and angry. I used to read some of the letters he wrote my mother then—he'd make as if he just moved through everything, moved through the streets, the night, fires, rubble, people. He and a gigantic

Scotsman called MacAndrew who worked with him were walking home late after a raid, he'd write, and MacAndrew, "who then smelled beautifully of whisky," had fallen out of sight into a hole in the street. "The hole was a very large one, containing interesting rocks, and which led in turn to a tunnel, which led into the deposit vaults of Barclays Bank. MacAndrew, being Scots, refused to leave, and I, being Armenian, felt unable to persuade him. I enclose clippings of the arrest." He was often very tired, he used to write, and sometimes afraid, and "on dark nights have other dark thoughts I cannot name," and that was the most he used to give away in those days of his own feelings about it all. And then when the bombing had quieted down a bit, had quieted down considerably, seemed to have stopped—well, it's hard to understand how these things can happen, but of course one knows how they happen, they happen every day, in every country—on one such day, in early 1944, a "question" was raised in the House . . . as to why a person of "foreign ancestry" was in "these crucial times" allowed to occupy such a "key position" in an industrial city; and shortly afterwards he left. There was no other course. He left, and went back to London, where he tried to get something to do in one of the Information Offices, but things apparently were rather sticky for him, his "situation" had suddenly become rather sticky—it must have been a small nightmare. I mean, he really

cared. He had cared a lot. And so he packed, and
got himself a bunk aboard this freighter, this Brazilian freighter, and went finally off to join his family.
Forty-eight years old. No money (the little he had
left being "blocked" in England). The memory of a
flashing career. His wife and children living out of a
small apartment-hotel off Madison Avenue. He was
quite marvelous even so. Tired, marvelous. But then
he worried about the money. My mother had since
come into a little, a small trust from her mother,
which in fact was what we lived on. A few days
after he landed in New York he had taken my
mother out to dinner, to the Colony, I think—the
first time both of them had been together that way
in a long time. It had been nice, I gather. Big fusses
made (he'd known old Gene Cavallero from before
the war). Champagne. The works. The next morning he woke up in high spirits, and announced
plans to take a half dozen people to "21" for dinner
that evening, and my mother then told him that they
just couldn't do that sort of thing any more. He
went out that noon, went down to "21" in fact,
feeling terribly serious and solemn, and full of all
sorts of resolves about economy—a last drink at
"21" or some such, where he ran into Louis Mayer,
whom he had known when *The Green Hat,* his big
novel, had been made into a movie in the late 1920's.
They had lunch together. There was a whole crowd

of people, I gather, and lots of booze, and talk, and at some point Mayer leaned over and asked my father what he was planning to do. "I was just talking to Sam Goldwyn . . ." my father began, which was true—he'd met Goldwyn outside in the lobby and Goldwyn had advised him to buy race horses. "How much did he offer you?" Mayer asked quietly. My father thought for a moment. "Not enough," he said. "Would you take fifteen hundred for thirty weeks?" Mayer asked. My father said yes, and went home that afternoon, and called up lots of people to go out to dinner, and told my mother that he was now a screenwriter for M.G.M. He left for Los Angeles a few weeks later.

IT WAS MY FATHER who decided I should come out to California and join him just before Christmas. He was already working on a movie. Within a few days after his arrival there, to his surprise, to everyone's surprise, they had put him onto a movie—it was a William Powell, Hedy Lamarr movie, in fact, that was already in production and that some other writer had been messing around with. He sent letters and phone calls back to New York that made it all sound very busy and glamorous. He said he missed everybody. He said he didn't know if he'd be able to get home much before Christmas, and then hit on the idea that I should come directly out there from school. We would have a reunion, he said. Good times.

The train took me out to California that December, a bright cold East Coast December. Bleak Chicago. Servicemen everywhere. I had heard stories of the resplendent private cars of movie tycoons, and looked for them on the sidings, but they were nowhere to be seen. I sat up for nights and days looking out the grimy windows at the clean spare Western states. I was fourteen years old, and rode beside a young Air Corps captain returning home to Idaho, who answered my questions about airplanes and showed me pictures of his parents and girlfriend. There was a woman too, a girl, she must have been twenty-three or so, Ann Sheridan hair—the diningcar captain had seated me across from her the first night out of Chicago, and I found her very beautiful and fell in love with her the instant she laughed at one of my stories, or whatever it was that I was telling her. She took my hand at one point, or so I thought, or so I remember. I spent the rest of the trip searching for her about the train, but when I found her she was usually seated in one of the club cars with other men, or groups of men, not laughing usually, just sitting. Once I remember going by her, some sort of colonel was holding one of her hands, and a man in a business suit had an arm across her shoulders.

My father met me at the station in Los Angeles.

I didn't recognize him at first, which was okay, he was still far away, with one of those wide-brimmed dark hats he used to wear. Everything was smaller, less than I'd expected. California was smaller, less, and he too. My *father,* I wondered, knowing full well that this man advancing down the platform was inalterably my father. Arms outstretched. A sudden wave. We hugged. He had tears along his face. This stranger. I hugged him hard, harder. This stranger. I kept looking at him, trying to do so in a way that wouldn't be evident. We walked, the two of us, back down the platform. How big you are, he kept saying. How well you look. How is everything at school? I answered dutifully, trying not to be dutiful. He seemed so small to me, I hadn't realized he was so small, no taller than I was really. We went outside and took a taxi to the hotel, the Beverly Wilshire. I have a room for you, he said, just down the hall from me. I let him propel me about. Hotel clerks. Bellboys. The Beverly Wilshire seemed dark and garish, and I felt myself withdrawing, withdrawing all the time, not wanting to—wanting to be there. Breakfast, he kept saying. You must be hungry. I said I wasn't. Of course you are, he said. We'll have breakfast together. Shall we have it up here? he asked. Or shall we go downstairs? The dining room isn't much, he said. You should have seen the food we had in England, he said, when the waiter and table arrived. Everything is amazing here, he said. The Americans are amazing. I looked at him across the hotel table in that hotel room. I didn't mind hotels. There had been that hotel in London. Each winter, for a few weeks after Christmas. Cold winds outside. Inside, the smell of porridge. One called it porridge. Wheeled in on a large table. Gaiety. Warmth. My father had been there too, in the next room in fact. And now here he was. This man. His mustache was thicker than I'd remembered. I spoke to him about my school, and said "thank you" a lot. He seemed not to notice any of it, although once he suddenly reached out his hand across the table and clasped me, and I tried to clasp him back, and there was something in his eyes just then, but I don't know what it was.

We went out that afternoon to "the Studio." M.G.M. Culver City. He had a limousine for us. They sent a limousine for him every day, he said. It was part of his arrangement with Mr. Mayer. He made it all sound very posh and debonair, and I felt better as we drove. The studios were big. Impressive. Great white and gray buildings. Sheds. Lots of people. We drove on through the gate, and over to a large nondescript building, where the offices were, he said. I got out and thought that we would go up together to his office. I was curious about what his office might be like, having read somewhere about Selznick, or was it Zanuck, having an office full of tiger skins and elephant tusks, but he said for me to wait downstairs, he would be back in a moment. It was a ramshackle sort of building on the inside, narrow corridors, pasteboard walls. Men and a few women, none of them beautiful, passed in the halls, greeted each other. My father seemed uncertain of his way. I hoped people would greet him too, but they didn't. I waited by the guard's desk while he disappeared upstairs. He came down again in about ten minutes. "We'll go and watch some of the shooting," he said. "Nothing's open today," said the guard. We went out anyway. My father was talking about the techniques of "special effects," but as far as I could see only for my benefit. He was telling me about a scene in an Errol Flynn movie that was then being filmed, about how they used a great tank of water, and wave machines, and had all these ship models—he was walking beside me across the M.G.M. lot, smiling, discoursing about this tank of water, and Errol Flynn. Errol is an old friend, he would say at several points. We walked between sheds, around sheds. People all around. We looked into buildings. A few sets were open, but nothing was happening. There were lots of actors in Navy uniforms on an empty stage. Lots of cameras. I had this feeling that neither of us could stop walking, that neither of us knew how to stop walking. He asked a guard where the tank of water was that they were using for Errol Flynn's movie, but the guard appeared not to know anything about it. "For Mr.

Flynn's picture," my father repeated, as if the "Mister" would somehow set it straight, but the guard was having none of it.

We walked some more, in a kind of desperation, so it seemed, and then we went on back to Beverly Hills. I felt he must surely want to get rid of me, for a while anyway, but he kept thinking up things to do, things that neither of us much wanted to do. Have tea. Go to some sort of movie museum. I suddenly realized that it was I who wanted to be off, and hated myself for feeling that. I said something about being tired, and went to my room anyway, and lay stiffly down on the bed for a few minutes, hoping indeed that I might be tired. But then got up and went downstairs and out of the hotel. The sunlight seemed very yellow, glaring, just then. Palm trees in the sidewalk. Careful lawns. Small genteel shops. Beverly Hills in those days wasn't so different from what it is today. It was all of it, anyway, a new world. America. The school in New Hampshire was America, with all its fine-looking, athletic, confident, East Coast boys, their settled houses, their settled families, their settled talk of summer places. Going-on-to-college. Parties in winter. And here clearly was America too. The tanned open-shirted men. The palm trees. Motion. Big cars and slangy waiters. The assumed assurance everywhere. I thought of my father upstairs in his room. I couldn't fit him in anywhere, which troubled

me—for thinking about it in the first place. I went
back into the hotel later, not wanting to go back in,
and we went out to dinner. I kept hoping that things
would somehow get better—I don't know what I
wanted from him. I had told myself that I hardly
knew him, had only memories. I knew that he was
kind and loved me. I knew that from memory and
instinct, I suppose, and what I wanted was to love
him. And so we went out to some place like Chasen's.
No, Romanoff's that night. Mike Romanoff. Another
"old friend," who actually did seem to be a friend.
There were some other people with us, Bill Hartwood, a screenwriter, and his wife, and then some
others, two men and a woman. The woman's name
was Mrs. Danvers. My father kept referring to her
as Mrs. Danvers. She had that Lana Turner blond
hair, and body, and a nice distracted smile. She
asked me about school. Everybody asked me about
school—they would periodically interrupt their own
conversations, which were mostly stories, anecdotes,
to pause, and lean over, and ask me about school.
My father was being very funny, I could tell. Bill
Hartwood and Mrs. Danvers laughed a good deal. It
pleased me, that. I felt taken aboard, at ease, and
then it suddenly all seemed to go wrong—somebody
else had been telling a story, one of those Hollywood stories that I think I still dislike even now as
much as I did then (some last remnant of primness,
I guess), what used to be called a dirty story, but

which seemed somehow different there, more than that. Nasty. I can't explain it much beyond that. There was a burst of laughter anyway, and then my father started to add to it, to extend the story, but nobody was paying him any attention. It wasn't as if they were pointedly ignoring him, it wasn't as if anything very definite was happening, had happened. There he was, telling this story or whatever it was (a starlet story, I remember, although I've never been able to remember anything more), trying—it seemed suddenly and awfully—to be like *them,* and being in the end so different. Not enhancingly different. Just different. Invisible. I hated him for tagging onto that story, and I think I hated him even worse for seeming just then so different from all the others. And I began to look for this, this difference between him and all the rest—it seemed so like a threat to all of us, my family. And I felt awful about it—I know it sounds self-serving to say that, to be self-protectively demanding of someone else and then say one feels badly about being so, but that is how things were. I had felt so often (and unwillingly) like a spy in the world, in the several worlds I had entered, halfway entered, been nudged into; and now I felt like a spy with my father. I don't know what he felt with me, but I knew it was not working out well, my visit, his idea. Our reunion. And it was to go on for seven more days—I truly dreaded each of them. And something began to build

51

up inside him too. Maybe impatience at me, which he couldn't accept, and which anyway took the form of worrying that he wasn't showing me a sufficiently "good time"; and so he started taking me around even more, more dinners at Romanoff's, Chasen's, more producers, parties, stories, that kind of hard-baked, crackly, ungiving laughter that I still associate with Southern California, although I haven't heard it there for over twenty years.

We were to go out to Santa Barbara that week-end—Clark Gable had a place out there. Clark was an "old friend." We went on out. The limousine. An hour's or so drive up by the Pacific. My father very silent. We got there around Saturday noon. Gable was not there, in fact was not going to be there, but there were a number of other people. Tanned, tall Americans. A big Jewish producer. Women. Everybody seemed to be drinking. My father, I'd come to be aware, drank a good deal, but not usually the way they were drinking then, bottles of bourbon and Scotch set on the table, people pouring it into glasses. My father began drinking too. We were all sitting around inside. People talking, trade talk. He would start in to say something, take hold of something, try to take hold, some line of wit, or style, a curl of sentence, but nobody was interested. I could tell it. I didn't know if he could tell it. Nobody seemed interested in what he said, in him. Everyone nonetheless friendly, or whatever it is that passes for friendliness. They talked—it is hard now to remember what anyone talked about, but I have still a feel of that Saturday afternoon, a long afternoon it was too; the big pink house, the phony ranch, great lawns, and colored flowers; the sea somewhere around; a huge green pool; and everyone indoors, stuffed silky chairs, a glass-top table mounted on a piece of driftwood. Blond girls with beautiful lip-sticked mouths seated low around the driftwood table, smoking, giggling. The men sitting, sprawled, talking about movies, about real estate, about the Japs, about nothing really, everybody very languid, savvy. The war in the Pacific was still going on, although it was hard to tell. Someone said something about that—I forget again what it was. Something about bombing, the bombing of Germany, and my father suddenly, I remember, became very loud, unnatural. Angry, but the anger not seeming to have anything to do with anyone or anything in that room. And everyone was silent, the girls in their big lip-sticked mouths blowing out cigarette smoke, and looked at him. Cigarette smoke. And then somebody said, in that grunting offhand open-necked leathery way—he should have another drink and not take things too damn seriously; and then he was silent. He did take another drink, but he didn't say much of anything again, didn't even seem to be listening to the others, and then he left, walked out of the room. "A very well educated man," the Jewish producer said to me, in a confidential tone, after he had gone out. "A class writer, and clearly a very well educated man." I stayed on there around the table for a little while longer, trying at the same time to be part of the group and to be invisible, a difficult combination. One of the blond girls had moved up on the couch between two of the men and was kissing them alternately, neither of them paying much attention to her. One of the men, in a sort of absent-minded, slow-motion fashion, reached over and put a hand on her breast. "That's nice," the girl said. The man took his hand away and the girl looked at him and got back down off the couch. I found my father outside by the pool. He was sitting by the pool—it was one of those new fancy-shaped things, green tiles, a rubber raft was floating on the water. I sat down on the grass, beside his chair. "I was out here a long time ago," he said. "We used to play tennis. Thalberg—he always wanted to talk about literature." He put a hand on my shoulder. "I worry about you," he said. "I can't give you happiness but I want you to really know about things." He stood up. "I've missed you," he said. Then: "Let's go back in." He stood for a moment looking out across the cypresses at the sea. "You know, that's a very very boring ocean," he said, and we went back into the house, and said goodbye, and drove into town, and had dinner later that evening with Charles Brackett, a funny man, and Mrs. Danvers.

$\mathcal{T}$HERE ARE THESE PICTURES OF HER AS a girl. Fifteen or sixteen. Dark hair down to the shoulders, a girl's hair, young. Dark eyes. A nearly beautiful, becoming beautiful, face, although a little plump just then. "I used to be so shy as a girl," she once said. "You would not believe how shy." The girl in the photograph wears a long print dress, and stands between two small trees, real trees, some country place, the farm outside Athens perhaps. Everything is young in the photograph, motionless as in a studio—the trees, the lawn in front of the trees, everything is charming, civilized, fixed firmly in place, save for the look on the face of the girl, which is not a shy look.

There are other photographs. Later. The girl is

beautiful now, seems very far from girlhood. The
hair sleeked back. The eyes very proud. The face,
especially from the side, quite perfect. The dress is
now a bride's dress. White. The look on the face
dark, dark as a Spanish princess. And later the pictures with the children. Children on lawns. Children
in English clothes. Children on the beach. The woman's face is still proud, darker even. The eyes look
out, dark eyes, the face of a dark madonna. The
eyes are not a madonna's eyes.

MY MOTHER DIED when I was thirty-three. Her husband, my father, had died eight years before that.
She had never, it would now seem, really made it
in life, connected with the world; had connected
only with him, through him (his connection itself
so haunted and peripheral), and when he died, she
was left, a little like an astronaut cast adrift from
his spaceship and spinning slowly, slowly off into
the void; she herself spun wildly, angrily, with fits of
rage and bitterness, and drink, and pills, and complaints, and sickness—she who had never been sick,
now sickly, now suddenly prey to headaches, back-
aches, complaints, *complaints,* her body itself turning on her, the skin sagging not so much with age
as with malaise, the body swelling not from flesh or
fat but from something no longer tenable; she, too,

slowly slowly drifted off into her own universe—
somebody's universe.

It was such a lousy time for her—for me too,
really. But mostly for her. So much going wrong, so
much hidden in mist and vapor. All the sunlight gone.
There was this apartment, their "home" in New
York. They had bought it, she had bought it about
five years before my father died. A commitment to
the New World. A commitment to something. It
was on Park Avenue, Seventy-fifth Street, one of the
inner apartments, quite large, quite elegant in a way.
The crystal chandelier was brought over from Fiorentina and installed above the winding staircase. Furniture was brought over. Aubussons. Some Chinese
stuff. Their home. And, of course, while they were
getting it, arranging it, my sister and I were readying
to leave. We had our rooms, were given our rooms,
and my sister indeed kept and used hers for quite a
while, it was *her* room. But mine was never mine,
my rooms anyway had always been at schools, at
college. And the apartment itself had this dark,
heavy, morbid look. Even then, when I didn't think
about morbidity, at least not in the same way I do
now, it had this look about it. Things turned inward.
Things waxed over, covered. There was a photograph
she kept on her desk, a photograph of the two of
them seated beside a pool near Cannes, near Antibes
probably, both of them so young, glistening, nearly
naked in the sun, as naked anyway as the 1930's

would allow, glistening bodies, you could feel the heat and see the sun everywhere—the sun was nowhere around now, was not even looked for. The curtains always drawn. The beautiful curtains. The curtains were of some Veronese silk, and previously had belonged to Mama, and to Grandmama before her. The curtains were drawn every evening at five o'clock, and opened again when the maid made her rounds in the morning. Curtains. Carpets. And after he had died (had died upstairs at "home," made it a point to do so, was proud of that), she continued there, seated most every night in that sofa in the library, the right side of the sofa, *her* side, eyeglasses beside her on the cushion (she wore glasses now to read), a book open on the table but barely read at, often the television on but not looked at, sometimes with the sound off, a drink nearby. I would come by to visit, to talk and be dutiful, and she would rage at me—doubtless (among other things) for just that, for talking, or listening, and being dutiful. She would sit there on the far side of the sofa, her body which had once been so beautiful, slender, proud, now swollen, not immense, but swollen, stout; doctors kept finding various names for her swelling, for this expression of her body, "colitis" it was sometimes called, or "pancreatitis," as if naming it would somehow wrest some sense out of it. She would sit there and I would sit in the big chair opposite, and we would drink after dinner, and talk about this or that, some movie, something ordinary that had happened, once I remember it was about as harmless a subject as a recent speech of Conant's about education that she'd fastened on in the *Journal-American,* and then she'd erupt—a wild dark storm, a mad queen, the elegances gone, the water suddenly rising, the waves coming seemingly out of nowhere, the trees bending, straining, everything threatening to come apart. I had been selfish toward her. I had turned her aside, betrayed her. I never understood much of that then, don't understand much of it now—some things, psychiatry to the contrary, are not much, or usefully, amenable to understanding. But it was difficult then, difficult for both of us, and especially for her because at first the only way I knew to manage it was by making myself invisible. An act of self-protection, like all those other wretched acts of self-protection, of hiding oneself under the coverlet, the tarpaulin, as if the force that seemed to menace me was *in fact* a storm, a raincloud, a torrent, something out of nature, implacable—instead of what it was: another human, reaching out. Reaching out madly at times. But reaching out. Yes indeed, I would say, cool in my chair. Maybe, I would say. You have a point, I would say. *Vous avez raison. Vous avez tort.* A soft voice turneth aside harsh words. It seemed to me a civilized, grownup way to act, and probably was. And then one spring they found she had breast cancer, suddenly, the way they do. And so they

operated, and then said she was fine. She had some
X-ray treatments for a while that made her feel
rotten. Burned. But then all that stopped, she seemed
okay. Things quieted down between us in a way.
We even did things like have lunch together, although rather guardedly, each of us careful to keep
the conversation out of reach of the dark monsters.
And she loved my children, as grandmothers do, and
you could see in the raw passion with which she
sometimes embraced them a glimpse of the forces
that had often swirled up and out of her in her own
life; what one saw of her with her grandchildren
seemed more an intimation of what she was keeping
back, keeping unsaid—of the wildness that, as an
act of will, she kept *out* of most relationships, rather
than of what was still there, which was considerable.
And then one year later, feeling better, she decided
to spend the summer in Greece. She had been there
often in the recent past, she liked it, although in
many ways she now found it as alien as New York,
as alien as everywhere. The friends she had in Athens, it seemed, were really no more friends than
the friends she had in New York, an exchange of
handshakes between cripples. But the earth there
must have meant something. The place. The presence. Something more than mere memory anyway,
more than names in an address book, and chatty
lunches at Kefissia. I saw her off one evening at
the airport, late one evening, very late, the plane

delayed—we sat in one of those lounges and had a kind of dinner, and talked, nothing very much. It was fine. I suppose it wasn't "real"—a relationship sustained mostly out of memory. But cozy. Quiet affection. Friendly chitchatter. Minor fussings about my sister. Serious discussions about my four-year-old daughter and the proper age to be taught swimming or not. That kind of thing. Just nice, and then she left to get on the plane. I'd never got used to her looking thick, and neither had she, but anyway I watched her walking away down the corridor or tunnel or whatever out to the plane, she had on a rather sweet dashing hat, a feather in it I remember, and carried a huge bag stuffed with all sorts of stuff, a half pint of Scotch included—and turned to wave, the way one waves. But it was nice. I think that was really the last time I saw her. I say "I think" because I did see her later, two months later in fact, but by then she was nearly dead.

By then she was no longer thick. No longer with that strange stoutness. Everything now drawn in, brought in, reduced. Ah God I hate that diminishment of cancer. My sister, now in Athens, had wired me first, saying she thought something was going wrong. And then when I phoned my uncle (who lived there), he had said he thought something was wrong, but that the worst thing would be to "worry her," to do anything rash. Etc. One was never supposed to do anything rash. I took something like the next plane over there, and even then it turned out that she was nearly out of it. She had been staying at the Hilton in Athens, one of those crazy Hiltons, and the afternoon I arrived, my sister in tears meeting me at the airport, she was already being readied to be taken to the hospital, to a small clinic in fact, about a mile up the road from the hotel. It was August, the middle of the tourist season, which was big and blooming that year. The Hilton full of drip-dry suits and cameras and restless kids from Minneapolis, a lunatic sort of carnival. We went in, then all of us went back out again through the hotel lobby, the hotel management anxious to have us out of there (a death in the hotel! an imminent death in the hotel!), that part of it so grisly I don't remember even noticing it, just remember one's feet clicking across the marble lobby, the attendants struggling with the stretcher. The hot hot air outside in the street. Hot and full of dust, and something else in the air that felt like chalk.

She could barely talk by then, my mother. She lay in bed in this clinic, which was a pleasant one really. The nurses were nice. Little Greek country girls. And she would sleep most of the time. They called it sleep, but it didn't have much to do with sleep. She lay there and disappeared, was disappearing, and now and then would emerge, eyes opening, looking out, even smiling, as if she had just been trying something out, practicing something for awhile, and now was briefly back. She lay in bed there I don't know how many days, three or four I think, the days seemed to merge into one another. She was so frail and thin by then, her face so thin, as if something inside her had been sucking everything in—something inside her which one could now almost visibly see, the belly swelling, the belly hurting. They gave her drugs now. She seemed in a state of constant dreaming, but then periodically would wake up, as if to surprise us with the unsurprising fact of her vitality. One afternoon old Nico came by, Nico Baltazzi. A large, cheery, stolid-faced Athenian. An old friend of my mother's, an old beau. I told her that Nico was outside—she was asleep, half asleep, but I wanted to tell her anyway. She woke up instantly. He can't come in right now, she said. Tell him to wait a few minutes, she said. And bring my bag. And so I did, both things, told Nico to wait, and brought the bag, and then she made herself up. She had barely the strength to hold the compact. It sounds perhaps a bit grisly, it wasn't grisly. It was quite marvelous. They were old friends, she and Nico, going back, way back. First parties. First dances. Nice Nico (he had recently married a fine English girl, after his first wife's death). He came in then, on "command," and they talked, or rather, he talked and held her hand, and then a while later he left, tears streaming down his big face.

63

Good tears, though. And hugged me. I remember
Nico's visit, but not much else about that time.
Hours passed. Relatives were around. Her sister, my
aunt, flew in from Geneva, full of distress, and an-
ticipated grief, someone who had already seen the
burglars prowling outside the house and whose mind
had then gone rushing on to counting up the expected losses. My sister was there too, being nice,
trying hard even now to please my mother, fetching
and carrying little things that my mother was too far
gone by then to care about. I spent a lot of time
then opposite the clinic at a small outdoor bar-café,
drinking that watery Fix beer, trying vaguely to read
Greek newspapers. And walking back and forth between the clinic and the Hilton—the Hilton which
seemed to have no connection to anything beyond
itself: an interplanetary object. And mostly at the
hospital, watching my mother who was dying, was
nearly dead, who lay there on the bed, propped up
on pillows; pillows on all sides of her so that she
would not move too much (because, when she moved,
her belly caused her pain), her face seeming now
so small, the hair which had been worn for much
of her life in that brave sweep atop her head, now
tousled, all askew, the hair of someone who has
been sleeping on it for too long. The room was
whitewashed white, a nice white. A nice room. The
air was hot everywhere, even inside the clinic, which
was air-conditioned, but imperfectly. A Greek sum-

mer. The clinic doctors had round calm faces. The nurses had thick legs and deep curling girlish smiles. Life amid death—and one could sense the impatience on everyone's part for death, could begin to feel it in oneself. We were waiting for her to die. There was no way left but that she would die (we were all sufficiently secular in our faith to thus accept the word of science), and bit by bit one could sense this invisible unspoken expectation begin to close in, to hover above us all. It was quite terrible to realize that. This woman lay upon the bed, my mother, my sister's mother, my uncle's sister, our kin, our flesh; and now and then she would struggle back from that far land she for the most part lived in now, and look at us, whoever of us was by her bed, my sister, myself, my uncle, a niece sometimes, the doctor (he was a kindly man, an Egyptian émigré, who told us stories about Farouk), her eyes half open, and smile, smile up, almost a girlish smile, not exactly of hope, of something else, beyond hope, and less insistent. And whoever of us was there would stroke her hand, or place cold cloths upon her forehead, and speak words to her, smile, and she would go back to sleep—and later we would gather outside the door. How is she? She seems comfortable. She is resting nicely. She had some broth today. She is less fevered. The phrases of concern, the technicalities of care and treatment would clatter back and forth between us, and all the while the expectation of

death hovered in the air, and we breathed impatient-
ly.

The day before she died, she virtually went to
sleep, as if she had already gone so far away, had
all these past days, while we sat about, and milled
in the corridor, and brought water, and held her
hand, had all these past days been quietly taking all
her baggage, suitcases, mysterious possessions over
to this far place, and now that she had everything
safely over there, she had no longer need to be back
here, with us. She went away, she was away, although still leaving behind something: the woman in
the bed. The woman in the bed, propped between
pillows, small head on the pillows, the skin on the
face now parchment-thin, the breath coming in great,
strangely rhythmic gulps of the warm air. And then
she woke up once, as I was sitting beside her, my
hand on her arm, an effort of will to make my hand
a living presence, not one of those damned gestures.
She looked at me with open eyes, and smiled, and
stroked my hand, such a feathery bony hand hers
was; and then she closed her eyes, and said: "Let's
take the road down by the sea this time. It will be
longer, but nothing really starts until ten anyway . . ."
and smiled, and fell asleep; and I realized that she
had just then gone way way back, her body mis-
shapen now by aging and disease, the glistening
dark skin now yellowing and hurting, all the hurts
of the last years, all the miseries, the not-compre-

hending, she had gone back to some evening when my father and she were young, and in love, and happy, and spun with the world, their feet in place, their bodies light; and on that particular night were driving out to Monte Carlo, because that was the road she most liked to take, the road by the sea. There have been so many times when I have railed and wriggled out of being taken for my father's son, my father's second; but then, just then I felt how cruel of life that he should not have been there himself, and also quite extraordinarily glad that it was me. And then she died, about fifteen minutes later. Without a sound. The nurse and I were talking about something by the doorway, and then she went over to the bed, looked at the still figure in the bed, and looked at me. All silence.

𝒯HERE ARE FOURTEEN BOOKS BY HIM, all in a row on one of the shelves in what real-estate agents would call my "library," but which in fact is just a fairly large wide wall of bookshelves. White shelves. From floor to ceiling. I used to like to keep books, to own books, a whole lot more than I do now. I can remember certain periods of time, school holidays and so forth, when the sequence between buying a book, reading it, and sticking it into a neat row in the small bookcase I had (a neat row full of captured prey) seemed wonderfully complete and satisfying. I used to buy books and read them just for this strange capture, and then later find myself looking at the books on the shelf, the trophies, with a sort of gloating; and feel terribly embarrassed; and go right out and do the same thing again.

But now I have all these books. They seem like a lot to me anyway. Some of them picked up when I was at school. Most of them bought, I think, at a time right after college when I went in for what must have been my final fling at the bookman's booklover's métier, running around to Village bookstores hunting up uniform editions of Conrad, sending away to Blackwell's in Oxford for a complete set of Forster. Once, sending away to Blackwell's for a five-pound slab of Wordsworth's *Prelude,* I can't imagine what in hell for. It sits there still, one of the very few books I own that I haven't read, or at least opened. My father's books are there, too—I put together a complete set of them after my mother died, my sister and I shuffling copies of *The Green Hat* and *May Fair* back and forth across the floor of the now-stripped library. A row of them, just above my uniform complete wonderful set of Conrad, and below some Greek and Latin prize books I received at school, and which I hang on to for mingled reasons of snobbery and affection and pride.

My father wrote a lot of books, it seems to me, in a short space of time, although I think it's true that novelists in those days usually did write lots of books. Certainly the novelists of those days whom he looked up to did, Wells, Bennett, Lawrence, and so forth. The first book my father wrote was called

The London Venture, a collection of sketches, London sketches, written in the first person, about a young Armenian (the narrator) called Dikran, who is trying to make it in London, and in the course of things has several highly talkative affairs, or encounters, with girls with names like Nadine and Shelmerdene. My father's name was then Dikran, Dikran Kouyoumdjian. At least it was when he submitted the manuscript to William Heinemann, the publisher, who said he'd take the book but advised that my father change his name—a change I think he was fully pleased to make, he was never much for Armenian ethnic pride, at least not when he felt it limiting. The book came out under the name "Michael Arlen," a name he'd made up (and had then checked out through all the available international phone directories in the Post Office Building to make sure there weren't any other Arlens anywhere else; there weren't in 1919). A strange-seeming name at the time, a strange-seeming book, rather more fin-de-siècle Paris than postwar London; at least more George Moore than Wells or Bennett. Some people actually thought it might be George Moore under a pseudonym, and in fact Alec Waugh, Evelyn's elder brother, a kind warm man who became a lifelong friend, reviewed it as such. "Is This George Moore?" (After my father's death, my mother gave Alec his big astrakhan coat, the fur collar still intact, and it is both a bit odd and very nice to still sometimes walk beside this coat, Alec inside it, down from the Algonquin after a lunch.)

The London Venture did all right in a modest way, its popular success probably not helped very much by the fact that my father's brother-in-law, Marco, in a typical fit of Armenian help-thy-kin-if-it-kills-thee-both gesture, decided one fine day, as a really nice nice thing to do for Dikran, poor literary Dikran, to buy up all the available copies of his book; and did so; and suddenly there were no more. My father never found out what happened to that speedily (and mysteriously) disappearing first edition until twenty years or so later when he received a letter from some warehouse in Buenos Aires, where Marco had "business interests," saying that they were still keeping all these crates of books for him, and what please would he like to have done with them.

It was a nice book, I always thought, that first one. A small book. Nothing very grand. Straightforwardly written, almost gentle. And I guess maybe what I mostly like about it still is that it's the only thing he published (that I know of) where he ever set down anything interior of himself—for all to see, for himself to see. To be sure, it wasn't the fashion then for novelists, or aspiring novelists, to write confessions or autobiographies. Novelists wrote *stories*. Works of fiction. I can even remember my father telling me, in a manner I always felt he

71

must have picked up from Wells or somebody, that no novelist worth his salt, no novelist who could tell a story, ever put *himself* too much into his own books. For me anyway, there were nice things in that first book. Small things. About living alone in London. About wanting success. About what it felt like to be a foreigner, to feel like a foreigner, in England—some almost very passionate things about that; I say "almost" because although there is anger and passion in a few places where he talks of being an Armenian in Anglo-Saxon England, the anger and passion remain mostly as hints, as coloring, are in the end kept tame in a context of amusingness. "An Armenian in London finds quickly that his nationality is something of a *faux-pas . . .*" and so forth.

The London Venture came out in 1920, when my father was twenty-four years old. He had no money then (and didn't make any to speak of from *The London Venture*), and lived alone in a small room above a shop in Shepherds Market, and worked like hell. I used to talk, or rather listen, to some of the friends who'd known him then, the few surviving, who'd tell me how carefree and debonair my father was in those days, how although everyone knew he had no money he was always showing up at "the best places" in "the company of beautiful women," and so forth. I really don't doubt either of those things, certainly not the beautiful women. I don't doubt any of it. But, my God, he was so ambitious. He was this young, slight, short, foreign-looking man, dark hair, long nose, dark face—and intelligent, talkative, nervy, and desirous to please in that endearing and awful way of certain foreigners in a strange court. His family were these small businessmen. Armenians, merchants, who now lived around Manchester and Liverpool. His father and mother, old people in rimless glasses and black clothes, who could still barely speak English; his three brothers and sister—the brothers already small businessmen since infancy: textiles, import-export, jobs in banks, little brick houses, not poor mind you, not rich, certainly not rich, above all cozy, semi-ethnic, little back-gardens dotted about Lancashire. His father, whom I've only seen in photographs (stolid, white-haired, a marvelous Levantine face), had taken the family out of Armenia at the time of the first Turkish massacres, had stopped en route in Bulgaria, where my father was born and the family ran a sort of general store, and then three years later headed for England. My father was the youngest brother. The other brothers had all gone into the family business, or anyway into business. My father was supposed to do the same; went to a second-run boarding school called Malvern; and then, in a final fling at career responsibility, or trying to please his parents, went off to the University of Edinburgh to study to be a doctor, got fed up after three months,

73

quit, and headed down to London. He wrote book reviews. Journalism. Some pieces for a new magazine called "The New Age." *The London Venture*. He knew he had something. He didn't know what at first—it was Lawrence, he said, who nudged him into the kind of fanciful writing, the kind of fanciful vision that eventually formed books like *The Green Hat* and *May Fair* and *Young Men in Love*. He used to go down to the country to visit Lawrence, he would tell me. When he was very young, and deferred to Lawrence greatly. (Lawrence, in fact, later wrote him into *Lady Chatterley* as Michaelis.) He would bring him stories that he was working on, and read them aloud to Lawrence, who would offer his advice. For quite a while, before *The London Venture,* he had been trying to write "realistic" Bennett-type stories, and hadn't been having much success. One weekend, he showed Lawrence a new thing he had been working on, a romantic, highly stylized fable about a girl (which later became one of the sketches in *The London Venture*). Lawrence, with all his didactic authority, said that Dikran should obviously stop trying to imitate Arnold Bennett, and should write fantasies. Or something like that. My father, at any rate, was always pleased to say that it was Lawrence who turned him towards his particular style, probably because it was partly true (Lawrence, I think, did take a genuine interest in him), but more probably because he liked to have been to some degree friends with these titans he so much admired, the serious literary men, the Lawrences and Wellses and so on. I remember once my mother describing to me how he had taken her round to meet H. G. Wells shortly after their marriage. They were to have tea or something. And my father so nervous. Fussing a lot beforehand. Changing his clothes several times—not dressy enough, too dressy? And then, once he got there, all nerve and suaveness. My mother said that Mr. Wells was very "dear" to her, and that my father did most of the talking.

Anyway, after *The London Venture,* he began to write like hell. The personal, alienated, young Armenian of the sketches disappeared, and was supplanted by the sisters and brothers and friends of the young Armenian's fantasy girls, Shelmerdene and Nadine and such. Lots of short stories—about silly young Lords, who drink champagne in the morning, and marvelous new 1920's women, who swear (ever so slightly) in public, and are bored with silly young Lords. The writing very mannered, in places wonderfully mannered, full of wit and elaboration (very exotic, people would say; very "Arabian Nights"), in places too full of curlicues and overwritten. But something new. With lots of style. Books of short stories called *May Fair* and *These Charming People.* Romantic novels with titles such as *Piracy, Lily Christine, Babes in the Wood,* most of which are right on the edge of romantic melodrama (and some,

75

it's always seemed to me, which are right over the edge). And then there was *The Green Hat*. He wrote *The Green Hat* when he was twenty-seven years old. He'd gone back up to Lancashire one summer to visit with his parents—stayed there two months, in the little house in Manchester, and in the course of that time wrote a novel. It began as follows: *It has occurred to the writer to call this unimportant history "The Green Hat" because a green hat was the first thing about her that he saw: as also it was, in a way, the last thing about her that he saw. It was bright green, of a sort of felt, and bravely worn: being, no doubt, one of those that women who have many hats affect "pour le sport."* It was enormously romantic. And lushly written. And very "modern" (in a way that few popular novels had been up to then), in that it at least admitted the possibility that men and women sometimes had affairs outside of marriage, and dealt more or less openly with such non-drawing-room matters as syphilis—handsome, dashing Boy Fenwick ("the most gifted of God's creatures"), who marries the heroine, beautiful Iris March of the green hat, commits suicide on his wedding night because of having had syphilis. In the end, much later, having all along been in love with somebody else, Iris kills herself by driving a Hispano-Suiza into a tree. The moment he'd finished writing it (he said later anyway), he knew that it was going to be a popular success.

Success—all the years I knew him, he had this am-
bivalence towards success, intensely wanting it, then
seeming not to care about it at all. He used to speak
of the mixed, unsettling feelings that he'd had when
he realized, first from his publisher's enthusiasm,
later when the book came out and had started to
take hold, that somehow, more or less by chance
(although not entirely by chance), he had happened
to strike one of those chords that a very few writers
strike each generation, or semi-generation—and that
people out in the audience fasten on to with a kind of
hunger because the new sound seems suddenly to tell
them who, and where, they are. He loved the success
part. He loved having money, and being asked to
dinner with Otto Kahn, and buying speedboats, and
all that stuff. He was probably better equipped to run
gracefully with a lot of money than most young
writers have been. But there was this something else,
too, and I know it is terribly corny to remark of
so-and-so who has just struck oil, oh yes, well of
course he doesn't object to the fame and money,
but deep down he believes there is something more
important in life than mere riches, etc. The thing is,
my father wasn't like that either. I think he loved
the glitter, popular recognition (such of it anyway as
he had), embraced it, and at the same time was
coldly detached from it, as if knowing all along that
there was something within him he ought to be taking care of, but not really knowing what it was,

saying in fact, well if I don't know what it is, it can't be that important. But my guess is it probably was, although that is only a guess, and a son's guess at that.

I think I would have liked to have known him in *The Green Hat* period. When he was young, and full of dash, and neither quite a gentleman, and neither not; and he really did make quite a splash. It's hard, I think, for people nowadays to realize about things like that then. Nowadays, there are seemingly hundreds of people so well known or publicized for one reason or another that their names are household words. But then the celebrity business hadn't been around very long. The 1920's more or less invented it. Channel swimmers. Movie stars. Even writers. It hadn't been all that long ago that writers, in England at any rate, weren't really allowed out of the kitchen. Writers were as bad as journalists, usually worse, since some journalists at least had power. Today, of course, writers are not only out of the kitchen, they're all over the house and in most of the bedrooms. But then—I don't know much firsthand about it, but later on, when I was at college, and my mother had brought a lot of our old things over from the South of France, I used to come in late sometimes and look over the scrapbooks that he or his publisher had kept of those years, the late twenties. Reviews. Photographs. News-

paper stories. Mr. Michael Arlen has taken up golf.
Mr. Michael Arlen has left for Biarritz. Mr. Michael
Arlen is in Saint-Moritz. Mr. Michael Arlen has
signed a contract—with *Cosmopolitan,* which made
him at that point the highest-paid short-story writer
on either side of the Atlantic. The day he arrived
in Chicago, the *Daily News* ran a front-page story
—saying that he had arrived in Chicago. He was on
one of the early covers of *Time.* It must have been
a wonderful, strange world he moved in then. He
arrived in Chicago that morning, as it happened, for
the local opening of the play he had made out of
The Green Hat, which had been one of Katharine
Cornell's first big roles on Broadway. He was thirty
years old. Dark, brushed-back hair. A bristly mustache. A marvelous photograph on the Chicago
station platform, in big twenties hat and astrakhan
overcoat. "Mr. Arlen, what do you think of yourself
as an artist?" a reporter asked him. He paused for
a moment (the reporter wrote). "Per ardua at
astrakhan," he replied. He was very good at that
sort of thing. In those days, they named children
after him—at his funeral I remember standing in the
back of the church, and this family, this group of
people I'd never seen before, coming in the door,
walking down the aisle, man, woman, several children, clearly not from New York, not friends of his.
They were the Martins from Detroit. Her name—
she had been born in the late twenties—was Michael

Arlen Martin, and now she had brought her husband, and her whole family, to the funeral.

The Green Hat made him rich, although not as rich as most people seemed to think. He used to give out all these stories about the money. (Never believe what a writer says about how much he makes, he often told me later; he's nearly always lying.) People seemed so to want to believe that he'd made a fortune. One million pounds sterling. Half a million pounds sterling. In fact, it was a good deal less than that. There weren't all those paperback rights then, and although M.G.M. did make some sort of a droopy movie out of it, with Greta Garbo and John Gilbert or somebody, they certainly didn't pay anyone $500,000 for the property. He did okay, though, better than just okay. And you didn't have income taxes to worry about then. He could buy a long damn canary-yellow Rolls-Royce. And speedboats. And good clothes. Things like that. And he could afford to marry my mother, in the sense that they could take a fairly large nice house in the South of France. Have nice things. Invest in the stock market in 1928. Scott Fitzgerald came by one evening, hours late for dinner, striped blazer, white flannels, full of booze from one of Gerald Murphy's parties, embarrassed, garrulous, then silent, leaned his head down on the table top (hair halfway in the soup). "This is how I want to live . . . this is how I want to live," he said. And fell asleep.

THERE WAS THIS WHITE ROOM I remember. At the end of a long corridor. The walls in the room were all painted white. Blue curtains, a deep blue. Sunlight. A Persian carpet on the floor, a kind of brown and blue color. The big desk. Some chairs. Papers. Books. The smell of kippers in the early morning—a breakfast tray, silver and china, off to one side of the desk. I would come down the corridor after breakfast, after my breakfast, and knock on the door, and he would say come in, and I would go on in, and fuss with the papers, and fiddle with the paperweights, and do what is known as "saying good morning," and go on out again. The smell of kippers, and all that sunlight. It seemed a magic room. I had no real idea of what he did in there—writing. It seemed as if that must be a fine thing to be doing. He was writing books—those few books he wrote after his big successes in the twenties, and while the world beneath his feet and all around him was changing, and while he was changing too: *Man's Mortality. The Flying Dutchman. The Crooked Coronet.* Nobody liked them much. He liked some of them, or thought he did. *Man's Mortality* he liked a lot, he had a lot at stake in *Man's Mortality,* his first "serious" book, a futurist, slightly Huxleyan novel about life in 1980, when the world is being governed by a supra-national "air transport cartel" called "Airways." It was okay, too. It wasn't brilliant, it wasn't the best thing anyone had ever done. But it was an interesting book, and written with imagination, and with an intelligence that was only then finally beginning to take itself seriously. But nobody else much liked it. The people who had liked him for being so charming and amusing and elegant disliked him for trying to be serious. The people who had disliked him for not having been serious enough now disliked him even more for trying to be serious and for not being better at it. And then, to be sure, there was the swirl of the thirties all around, the thirties of the Depression and the disappearance of canary-yellow Rolls-Royces, the thirties which turned against Fitzgerald's *Tender Is the Night* as being irrelevant to the period. I think probably everybody had a point, everybody usually does. But I am thinking now of the man who wrote in that white room, that lovely white room, surrounded by all the things he thought he had finally achieved—fame being only a small part of it. A splendid wife, whom many admired. A son, a daughter. A family. A fine house. This room he wrote in, with its big Empire desk, especially built for him somewhere in Paris. A secretary, nice old Miss Livesey, who would come in during the afternoon, while he played golf, and transcribe his longhand into typescript; and then later, after golf, after a drink or so at the club or at the Carlton, he would come back in after dinner, and make a few corrections in the margins. Like that. It must have seemed a lovely life. It must have been a lovely life. I can remember sometimes, after lunch, my lunch, being driven down into Cannes beside him. He had this small sporty Ford then, a small black car, he at the wheel, myself beside him, the two of us gliding and winding down the roads out of the hills above Cannes, down towards the beach, the town, wherever. I can remember him singing—such an ordinary thing to remember. But I think I can remember him singing only once or twice in my life, and that would be once; in the car after lunch. Usually I would drive down with my mother, once a week or so, and we would go to the little nanny-packed beach in front of the hotels on the Croisette. A narrow strip of sand. Umbrellas. Old men selling peanuts. And then afterwards, sometimes, my mother would take me by the Carlton, the Carlton bar, and I would sit there quietly, and be given one-franc pieces with which to play a machine they had in there (you operated a kind of pincers and tried to pick up "valuable objects"), and wait for them until they were ready, he was ready, and we would all drive home together, back up the hills.

It seemed to me a marvelously happy time. Even now, looking back on it, having some sense of how the world was turning then, having some sense of

who the people I lived with really were, it still seems
a marvelously happy time. Full of light. And space.
And spaces between people. And water. He had a
speedboat then. The *Swallow II,* one of those huge
lovely mahogany. Gar Woods, with a pennant on the
front, and lots of brightwork, a windshield like a
racing car, and Rafael, a wiry, gleaming Portuguese,
who took care of the brightwork and the engine, and
who sometimes drove it—a speedboat chauffeur. In
the spring sometimes, we would go on afternoon ex-
cursions to the Ile Sainte-Marguerite, small islands a
little way off the coast, not really islands at all,
clusters of rock, outcroppings in the water, the *Swallow II* larumphing across the flat waters of the bay,
laden with hampers, satchels, my mother and father,
I, Rafael. We'd anchor off one of the larger rocks
and go swimming, all of us, my mother sleek and
purposeful with her bathing cap and sidestroke. And
later, just Rafael and I, the water beautifully clear,
green, so clear you could see right to the bottom
twenty or so feet below. Rafael would fill his lungs
with air and go down beneath the surface, down to
God knows where, whole minutes at a time; I tried
to follow him, a dark shape way down beneath me,
gliding above the sand and coral, but had no lungs
for it, and no stomach either. Once, I remember, he
caught an octopus, a tiny thing, not much bigger than
his hand, all white and quivering. He killed it against
the side of the boat, and then on the way back he

84

would grind it against the planking of the deck. "It makes it tender," he said. His hand and arm moving in a circular motion. The red-brown boat jumping across the bay.

And all the while my father wrote these books, wrote at these books in that lovely white room in the morning. And Lord knows what was really going through his mind. My mother told me many years later that one spring afternoon in 1936, I think it was, he came down after lunch, and said that he was leaving, that he couldn't stand things any more, and needed to be by himself, and left, and went away, took the train up towards Paris, then to Cherbourg, got aboard the *Aquitania* bound for New York— but then got off again at Southampton and came back home again. "He never told me what had been on his mind," she said. "I asked him later," she said, "but he kept saying, Oh it was nothing."

AND THEN YEARS LATER there was this other room; a darker room now. The desk was still the same, shipped over from Cannes after the war. The desk stood in front of the windows, which looked out directly onto a gray-brick building across Seventy-fifth Street, and which were always covered by curtains. The desk had on it all the artifacts of writing. Pencils. Paper. Notebooks. Pens. Ink. And around the walls of the room were books. The walls were painted

green, a darkish sort of green. My mother had
many wrangles with the painters over just the right
shade of green. There were some pictures on the
walls. Two Boucher little girls. Two prints of birds.
A watercolor of a hunting scene done very recently,
reds and whites on some kind of greenish paper. The
greenish paper went very well, she used to say, with
the green walls. The room was called "the library,"
and was in my mother and father's apartment in
New York, and it was where my father worked. Or
was supposed to work. Or tried to work. Or something. For years, since the end of the war, he gave
out all these airy stories about his not working, about
his being retired. I'd come down from college then,
sometimes on weekends, on vacations, and meet him
for lunch at the St. Regis, where he nearly always
lunched with friends, writers, editors, movie people,
vague acquaintances who would simply drop by there
around one o'clock or so, knowing he would be there.
From time to time some one of these would ask him
what was he doing. What was he doing? And he had
all these marvelous answers; his hard-working (or,
at any rate, employed) table-companions loved him
for these answers. I do nothing, he would say. I am
retired. I read a lot. He had little set speeches he
would sometimes make: "I have the affection of my
wife, the tolerance of my children, and the friendship
of headwaiters. What more do I need?" To reporters
and columnists (who still interviewed him despite

the fact he hadn't published anything in fifteen years), he stressed the financial aspects of his retirement. "The mistake most writers make," he would say, "is to declare that when they have enough money they will retire. Since they never have enough money, they never retire, and so poor Willie Maugham goes on grinding out book after book. I tried to be more modest. I said, when I have x-amount of money I shall retire. And, as things turned out, I eventually had x-amount of money. And retired. And lived happily ever after." He seemed to be living happily ever after too, although in truth I don't remember his having any friend close enough in those days to have known the difference. Nor any friend he would let that close to him. A great many people seemed glad of his company, always had been glad of his company. He really was a very good talker. Witty. Knew about a lot of things. Had opinions about a lot of things. Had style. Sitting there in the St. Regis. The elegant mustache. The English-tailored blue suit. The gray silk tie. The pearl stickpin. The malacca cane beside him. *Time* editors would come for lunch, and then agree—he really had the system beat. Why, he hadn't written a book in years and clearly was never happier. Better. Happier. Happier . . . And then later in the afternoon, I would come back home, back to their home, this dark elegant apartment, the Chinese screens, the fine-old-pieces, the chic little hallway, Grandmama's rugs, the whole place dark, silent—I'd go upstairs to what was supposed to be my room, get ready usually to go out again, sit in a chair for a moment reading a magazine, and from downstairs, just below my room, from the library I'd hear these footsteps. Footsteps pacing. Back and forth. It was a small room really, the library. I don't know how many thousands of times he must have walked around it. The big desk up against the curtains. The paper laid out for him. The pencils. His favorite pen. The books all around. He used to tell me sometimes that he "liked to pace," which in some ways was probably true. But for ten years or so he paced. No longer in that little room in Shepherds Market. No longer in that white white room, with the green of French hills around it, and a semicircle of the Mediterranean down below. Now there were all these books on the shelves above him, beside him, many of them his. Spanish editions of *The Green Hat*. Old George Doran editions. Leatherbound volumes of his earlier successes, which Heinemann's had done up for him at various long-past Christmases. He said, he used to say (he had this way of seeming so offhand about important things), that he was not really a writer, that he just happened to "turn to" writing, and maybe that was so, although I doubt it. I think of him still in those days, all those New York days, for there were a great many of them, pacing back and forth around that dark library. The walls must have seemed unbearably close at times. And then later, after dinner, he would seem so tired after dinner; he would sit in the big green chair in the corner of the room and read.

A CHRISTMAS IN SOUTHPORT: THE first winter of the war, which was also the first winter I'd been away at school (in Surrey, Abinger Hill), we all went up north to spend Christmas with my father's family, my Uncle Taki's family, who lived in a town called Southport, about a half hour or so from Liverpool, which was where Taki worked. My father's mother then lived with Taki, too (I think that would have been the last year she was alive). I don't remember much about her—a dear, small, old lady, seemingly always in black, and lace, and rimless eyeglasses, and with a smell of old flowers, strange kitchens, of something indoors about her, not speaking English very well, a penny apiece for each grandchild for being such good grandchildren,

plump white face, beads, warm warm eyes. My father would sometimes get impatient with her (he, the
youngest child), chide her for not speaking English
better, for not wanting to, for hiding behind her
foreign-ness. He would get impatient a bit with Taki,
but not really. Taki's actual name was Takvor. He
was the eldest of the brothers, a round genial man
who liked to play bridge in the evenings, and went
nine holes of golf each Saturday, in checkered plus-
fours out on the golf course near his house, a pleasant red-brick sort of residential row-house on the
outskirts of Southport. The war was just beginning
then, was three months old. Barrage balloons floated
above London. Antiaircraft gun emplacements in
Hyde Park. Sandbags. Soldiers in khaki and tin hats.
The air-raid wardens carried gas masks. Down
where I was at school, you could lie awake at night
and in the far far distance watch the slender beams
of searchlights poking around the sky. A German
boy called Schoenfeld, I remember, was given much
trouble in the locker rooms one afternoon. Several
hundred, or thousand, German paratroopers were
reported to have landed in nearby Abinger.

In Southport, everything seemed more peace-
able. Schoolboys in caps and shorts and jackets riding bicycles down the street where Taki's family
lived. Taki's two sons (my cousins John and Sarkis)
home from school, and playing Benny Goodman rec-

ords, that noisy American jazz, in the cellar. Taki going off to the bank each morning. Taki carving the roast at Sunday dinner. In the evening, Taki and my father would listen to the B.B.C. news, the hefty brown radio on the bridge table in the living room, and sometimes I would come in with them, lying on the floor with my cousin Sarkis's new edition of *Jane's Book of Fighting Aircraft,* and studiously subtract the announced losses, German, French, English, Polish, from the totals in the book. I was given a new bicycle. My sister took riding lessons, a small figure with frizzy blond hair, perched atop an enormous horse, going slowly round and round inside the wintry paddock. My father took me to the zoo. One afternoon we went to the movies. Disney's *Snow White,* the awful witch. My sister and I, my mother, and Anais, who was Taki's wife, a nice nice woman, who still lives in that same house today (as John and Sarkis live in nearby Manchester). I thought both Taki and Anais were very nice. The house had a good smell about it. Leaded bay windows in the front. Small garden out back, with flowers and little vegetables. And Taki, this marvelous Armenian, not trying to be English or anything as pushy as that. But English all the same, such a fine solid English voice, such fine solid English concerns. He had a reddish face, and a big-hearted laugh, and liked green, and gardens, and vegetables growing in the garden, and

small things in the fields outside in the special way
that only Englishmen do. Takvor Kouyoumdjian. He
was truly a very lovely Englishman. And he felt my
father to be something very rare too, and I liked
him for that. It wasn't that he and my father really
talked to each other much, talked about things,
about life, about careers, about God knows what.
But I can remember the way he sometimes looked
at my father, the way he'd say things, casual things,
the way we'd all go into dinner, his arm over my
father's shoulder. My father loved him back, although at times with prickles and impatience. My
father loved all his family, really loved them, really
cared for family, deeply extravagantly cared for *family,* as maybe only an exile can (or the child of
exiles), and also yearned, just yearned to be free of
them and glide above them. His two other brothers,
Krikor and Roupen. His sister, Ahavni, an extraordinary woman, short, tiny, bright red hair, full of
life and sex and gaiety, a really lived-in face.
Ahavni's husband Marco, who was considered family. They were all businessmen, not unsuccessful
either: small import businesses, and firms, and
holding companies all over the world. Buenos Aires.
Brisbane. Paris. Manchester. Montevideo. And each
with this special Armenian characteristic of being at
the same time enormously devious about business
matters, and enormously loving and loyal about family. All my father's family, as I think of them now,

seem so very warm, and almost childlike—oh, they
were tough as hell about business and textiles and
import-export or whatever, it was what they did in
Manchester and Montevideo; but in the interior of
their lives they were so unabashedly familial, tribal;
and despite how much they became parents themselves, had children, they remained, more than any
other people I've known, themselves children of parents. My father, I used to think, was the exception
to this, but I am not so sure. He handled it differently though. He made it look different; he made people
think he was the odd one, the one who broke the
rules, the one who had escaped, which was all true,
but it was not in the end, I think, an escape very
far down the road. He used to tell me how, when he
was married, at his wedding, in that chapel at Fiorentina in the South of France, an Armenian Ortho-
dox priest had suddenly turned up. Literally showed
up at the beginning of the service. Striding down the
aisle. Flapping black robes. Black hat. The beard.
He gave my father a knowing look, and whispered
in his ear that he had been sent all the way from
England by his mother, who feared that he would
not be married properly amid these pagan Mediterranean rites. He stood immovably a few steps behind
my father through the service. The Catholic priest in-
toned the Latin phrases. The Armenian muttered his
own in a just-audible chant. My father said it was
a ghastly experience, although he made it funny.

That Christmas his mother, I remember, gave me
a book about King Arthur. I was nine years old and
would have preferred *Jane's Book of Fighting Aircraft,* but I went upstairs to her room, where she
was in bed most of the time, and gave her a kiss
(she had hair on her cheek), and later read the
book, which was a good one. That Christmas. It
was a simple, friendly time. I think mostly of Taki's
laugh. And of John and Sarkis standing in the hallway in their long, schoolboy scarves. And of my
mother and Taki playing checkers after dinner,
which was something I had never seen her do. Our
other Christmases had nearly all been in Cannes—
one, I think, had been at a hotel in Vienna, but I
can barely remember it, except for people dancing,
and someone going about the corridors late at night
dressed as the devil. We'd have an enormous tree,
big enough anyway so that my mother and Monsieur
Puigue, the chef, would have to stand on a step-
ladder to hang the lights. Lots of decorations. Colored balls. My mother knew where each one ought
to go, packed them away in order, took them out in
order. A big party for children on Christmas Eve. My
father dressed up as Santa Claus, distributing pres-
ents from a large sack to dozens of mostly strange
children, who seemed to have materialized out of
nowhere. In Southport that winter, we sat around
the living room on Christmas Eve. And listened to

the B.B.C. Light Programme. And played round-robin checkers against Taki, who was very good, and won. The next day, Christmas, Taki and Anaïs gave me a flashlight, one of those long silvery things with lots of batteries, which would last for-ever. My mother and father, among other things, gave me a model airplane. I remember we put it together in the morning—it didn't take much, it was nearly assembled, an expensive bright-blue job from Selfridges. And my father and I took it out for a test flight in the afternoon. A cold gray afternoon. Gray sky. We went out towards the golf course. There was an aerodrome nearby, they called them aerodromes, a ragged wind-sock fluttering beside the runway. My father and I stood on a rise in the golf course, winding up the rubber band, tossing the little blue plane into the air. It was a nice one and flew quite well. Taki appeared. Those marvelous plus-fours, and wearing a checkered cap that Anaïs had given him for Christmas. He had a golf club under his arm. He'd been out practicing a few drives, he said. Taki took the plane, and wound it up, and tossed it into the air. It flew a few hundred feet and almost landed on a putting green. We all laughed. On the far side of the fairway, from off the runway, two R.A.F. bombers took off into the twilight—dark, bulbous, insect-like things. Jet black. The roar of engines. We flew the plane a few more times. Then Taki said: It's getting dark. It had already started to drizzle. A sea wind bringing the light rain in off the Atlantic. My father picked the plane up, and handed it to me. We walked on back. Taki between us. I held his hand. He had his arm around my father.

$\mathcal{N}$EW YORK IN JUNE. AT THE BEGIN-
ning of every summer we left New York—not so
much left it as flung ourselves out of it in the direction of some "resort" or other. At first, just my mother, my sister and I (and the inevitable tight-mouthed,
army-booted, Swiss governess); then later my father,
after his arrival from England. Apparently it was
something one did if one lived in New York. One
got the hell out by the middle of June. Trunks and
suitcases all over the apartment. Short tempers. Windows open in the New York heat. Soot. Sweat. Traffic horns. Why don't you children go out and play
in the park. Why don't you children go and roller-
skate on the sidewalk. Can we take our roller skates
to the country? No. Piles of clothes everywhere. My

mother striding about in her slip. "Where are your short-sleeved shirts?" I'd go rummage through my school trunk and reappear with a couple of wanly-colored cotton things. "How do you expect to get through the summer with these?" It didn't seem the kind of question that required an answer. The governess would bring in a black metallic suitcase, which I knew contained only walking shoes and chocolate, and place it in the middle of the living room. My sister would drag herself slowly down the hallway and stand in the doorway, modeling last year's riding breeches. My mother looks at her with a *Vogue* editor's eyes. Detached. "You're pushing your stomach out," she says. "I'm *not!*" my sister says. My mother walks over and tugs at the bottom of the breeches, presumably to see if they will stretch. My sister stands still, St. Joan at the stake, making faces. My mother sighs. Stage-right, the sound of a door opening. My father on his way out. "I'll be back later," he says. My mother dabs at her forehead with a handkerchief. Lights a cigarette. "What about your Palm Beach suit?" she says to me.

These resorts we used to go to were a sort of nightmare. Each year, it seemed, we went to a different one. Northeast. Edgartown. Once to New Hampshire: the White Mountains. For days on end we sat around this New Englandy inn. A swimming pool out back. Some tennis courts—the tennis pro had played (he claimed) number 3 on the Princeton team, which I thought was pretty hot. My father said: "All he ever talks about is drinking beer. He calls them brews." The year after that we went to Hot Springs. Hot Springs, Virginia. The Homestead. That huge white place. Long corridors. All those black slaves gliding up and down the carpeted corridors with trays balanced on their heads, those kinky woolly heads so justly famed in song and story. My father played gin rummy a lot. I took tennis lessons, from a leathery-faced Norwegian called Toby Hansen, who taught a nice straight backhand and what was then called an "Australian twist" serve. My sister was supposed to be taught riding, and was quite good at it, although my sister was not to be taken seriously. My mother went on walks, and also played tennis, and sat at table beneath the colored umbrellas of the Casino and watched while my father went into his fifth hour of gin with some Detroit industrialist. All around us the swirl of American girls and boys. Young men. Memphis. St. Louis. In other places they had been from Philadelphia. Boston. Long Island. Long-legged. Girls with breasts beneath white shirts. That summer I was in love with five different girls from Memphis, and spent much time in the swimming pool because all the girls from Memphis were in love with Allen Clayton, the swimming pro, a fair-haired muscular young man who had been something really terrific on the North Carolina swimming team, and who now walked up and down beside the pool with his beautiful tanned legs and beautiful white bathing suit. I had a dumpy blue bathing suit and wanted hugely to be like Allen Clayton. "Let's kind of take it a little easy there, old buddy," he would say. Later in the afternoon I'd go back to our room. "Let's kind of take it a little easy there, old buddy," I'd say to my sister, but she was usually in tears, or close to tears, because my parents were always threatening to cancel her riding lessons, and was never good for much response.

I could never really understand what we were doing there, or in any place like it. I knew one was supposed to go away from the city in the summer. I knew people went to "resorts." People *fixed* themselves in resorts. There were Edgartown families. Northeast families. Certainly Homestead families. My father and mother seemed rather to move through these places like émigré royalty, the innkeepers (and guests) vaguely conscious that somebody unusual was among them but not quite sure what currency they would be paid in, or when; my mother and father diffident, remote, not so much bored as disconnected, and with small gift for camouflage. I can remember us gliding into that wretched Homestead dining room each evening—it was one of those American resorts where the dining room was only open between some ridiculous hours like 5:30 and 7:30. My father in dark evening suit, well dressed, too well dressed, a boutonniere, a cane. My mother really

101

very handsome. Hair up high. Jewels. My sister and I trailing along, each conscious of the Detroit and Memphis eyes on all of us. And then would come the dinner scene: my father disdaining the relish tray. Each evening my father would disdain the relish tray, would look at it in fact, held in the hands of some hopeful moon-faced Virginia girl, some girl whom I would have paid money to like me—would look at it as if it were some joke that was being played on him, which in some ways of course it was, a joke to which he had been an accomplice (which must have made it worse). My mother (very regal, but trying to be creative): What are those little things in red? The waitress (not very bright, but trying to please; never run into this kind of rum crowd before): They're candied crab apples, ma'am. They come from right around Covington. A lot of the guests . . . My father (as if waking up): *Candied crab apples? For dinner? I should certainly hope not!* My mother: You've never tried one, Dikran. My father: I don't intend to. (Smiling sweetly, like a cougar, at the poor girl) Can you bring us an Old-Fashioned and a whisky right away? The waitress: Oh, I'm sorry sir. I'm only in charge of the relish tray. My father: Etc., etc. He and my mother would complain their way through dinner. I would squirm my way, conscious of every assault delivered by them against the system, which seemed a perfectly okay system to me (I liked relish trays, relish trays were wonderful, who would want to be so odd and alien as not to embrace a relish tray?); conscious that all their sniping and snipping was heading directly into some huge composite American ear, that would surely in turn spew maledictions back at me. Afterwards we'd usually all troop into the movie. The Homestead showed movies each night in its own plush little theater. And then my sister and I upstairs to bed. My parents to the lounge or some place, where they drank, and my father sometimes played more gin. "He usually had good cards," my mother used to say. She sat beside him while he played, reading a book, or smoking—to "bring him luck." The stakes weren't very high. I think he won a hundred dollars once. I hoped that some of the men he played cards with would become friends. All have dinner together. Get together "in town" after the summer. But it didn't seem to be that kind of a thing. Later at night, my sister and I would sometimes wander back through the hotel, hunting up groups of older boys and girls, but then she once got caught necking in the back lobby (I think it was just a kiss) with Foster Thompson of St. Louis, the riding teacher, and we were both confined to quarters for a while. I won a swimming prize in August, second place in the backstroke, but got no closer to the girls from Memphis. My sister went on a pack trip with her riding class. Towards the end of summer, a large family from Cleveland arrived. The

MacAllisters. Nice people really. Big bouncy unsexy girls. Everybody very tall, and tousled, and surprisingly gentle. And it turned out they were "old friends"—in the great long ago, somebody had once "played with" somebody, gone to the park, gone to birthday parties in Cleveland after the First War. Not very *close* friends. Still, it was nice. I hadn't known we were so American. We all went in to dinner together one evening. For a moment everything seemed wonderful, and I looked forward immeasurably to more.

$\mathcal{H}$ER NAME WAS AMY WELLS AND she said goodbye to me at the station. At Back Bay, just outside Boston. The train was late. It was one of those unnaturally hot spring days towards the end of May. She was wearing a hat that morning, I remember. A big straw hat. A yellow ribbon. It was really very hot. Her face was pink under the sun. And tense. We walked up and down a lot. We kissed. We walked up and down. Finally the train came in. There were a number of other people from college on the platform, a group of boys and girls who must have been freshmen or sophomores. Corduroy jackets and khaki slacks. The girls wore raincoats and smoked. They all seemed so young and full of good things to look forward to. I was twenty-one and felt horrible. "Phone me," Amy was saying. "Phone me right away." I said yes—it all seemed stifling, especially that "yes"—and got on the train.

New York in May. I should have taken a cab from the station and gone right home, but I walked instead, hot, sweaty, past the same shops I had walked by so many times before. I didn't want to go home at all. I knew that was weak, cowardly, that I was putting things off. Evading. I stopped at the drugstore on Seventy-fourth Street and had a milkshake, couldn't drink it. I went on home, remembering in the elevator that I hadn't told them I was coming. Teresa opened the door, tugging at her uniform. Oh, nobody told me you'd be down, she said. *They're* out, she said. Your mother will be back first. I began to pace around the empty apartment, suddenly crazy with impatience. I had to *do* something. I went into the library and tried sitting down in the big green chair, but that wouldn't work at all, I kept springing out of it. I snatched up magazines, put them down. I went over to the sideboard, fumbled together a drink, a bit because I wanted one, mostly because it seemed a serious and grownup thing to do, to pour a Scotch and soda down one's gullet at three in the afternoon. I heard my mother come on in. A rattling of keys. Sounds of parcels being put down in the hallway. I appeared out of the library, drink in hand. "Oh, it's you," she said. "Whatever are *you* doing here?" Suddenly my im-

patience vanished, mysteriously drained away. I
stood there in the hallway. Tense. Gray flannels.
Seersucker jacket. Probably gesturing vaguely with
my arm. "I just came down," I said. "Well, I can
see that," she said. Then: "Wait a moment." She
picked up the two or three packages and started
upstairs. "I have to get these out of their boxes." She
was halfway up the stairs. "I want to talk to you,"
I said. "What?" she called. "I said I wanted to talk
to you." She stopped and peered over the banister
at me, and then went on her way upstairs. I went
back to my drink in the library. The telephone rang.
I heard my mother answering it in the bedroom.
Some woman, Margot Humphreys it sounded like.
I picked up one of the magazines. I thought of Amy.
I thought of Amy's mother. I thought of the funny
smell of Amy's lipstick at the train station. I wondered what she was doing just then. My mother swept
into the library. She had changed into one of those
great flowing gowns. She carried her reading glasses
and the afternoon paper. "It's so hot in here," she
said. She swept on out and into the salon. I went
in after her. She was sitting in one of the two rose-
covered armchairs beside the window, leaning back
a little, she could have been tired, although I didn't
think she was. It was a nice room, really, pinks and
oranges and glass. She was doing something with her
hair, poking in or pulling out a pin. "Well, what is it
you consider so—" she began in that special voice

of hers. I couldn't stand it any more. "I'm planning to get married," I said.

Her face froze, unfroze, took on that unreal skeptical look. "Who are you planning to marry?" she said. I sat there opposite her, leaning forward, knees wide, barely sitting at all. She knew perfectly well who. "Amy," I said. "Amy Wells." She said nothing for a moment. "And what does Amy think about this?"

"Well, naturally she wants to get married. I mean, she's very happy. I mean, she wants to marry me." Oh God, that disjointed speech. I could feel those awkward, so inelegant, so uncontrolled, so adolescent stammers beginning to well up in me.

"Have you discussed this plan of yours with Mrs. Wells?" she asked. The voice soft, cool, an edge now on the word "plan." I sat back in my chair. Unclasped my hands. Crossed my legs, trying to look confident and casual and grownup. "Not in so many words," I said. "But I think she knows we want to get married and—" My mother suddenly rose to her feet, her face carved out of some dark stone. "If you've come to me for my approval," she said, "I absolutely will not give it!" I had never seen her eyes so full of temper. "You must be out of your mind!" she said, almost yelling. "You're only a child."

"I'm not a child," I said. "I'm twenty-one."

"Twenty-one," she said. "I'm not going to stand by while you ruin your life."

"I am not going to ruin my life," I said. "I love her. We love each other."

My mother seemed to peer at me as if I had just changed shape. I stood beside my chair. "Amy Wells!" she said. Then: "You're both children." She was really beginning to cry. And: "I thought you were more intelligent than that."

Later. In the library. My father still not back. My mother at the far end of the sofa trying to read the *Journal-American*. I stand in the doorway. I sit down in the big chair. My mother turns a page in the paper. "I don't care what you say," I say suddenly. "We're going to get married anyway." My mother glances up from the paper, looks over at me. "Do you have to get married?" she asks.

"What?"

"Do you *have* to get married? Is this Amy of yours pregnant?"

"No!" I yell wildly.

"Well, that's something," my mother says.

Dinner. My father arrived home just in time for dinner that night. He'd been with John McClain at the St. Regis. He talked about John, about John's new wife. The three of us around the oval dining table. The usual chicken broth. Toast. Teresa tottering around with little slices of veal. The usual rotten gravy. Once I caught Teresa's eye. She made a strange clandestine grimace at me. Intended-to-reassure. Teresa and I locked in a conspiracy. My father seemed blithely unaware of what had been going on, my mother seeming to refuse to recognize that anything indeed had gone on, everything apparently in its place, except that my mother had slightly red eyes, and I probably did too, and felt sick to my stomach. Towards the end of the meal, my father (who had seemed quite unsurprised to find me at home) finally asked me some innocent question about exams or some such. "I don't imagine," I heard my mother say, "he's had too much time for examinations lately." The battleship *Schleswig-Holstein* had evidently moved into place for the shelling of Dresden. My father predictably said "Oh?" and looked at me (I sat at table between the two of them), and while I sat there thinking of what precisely to answer, what best to answer, which of the seemingly eight hundred possible answers to nudge forward onto the tablecloth, the guns of the battleship all swiveled into place, the guncotton was rammed down the barrels, the fuses lit, the sailors all running back for cover . . . "He's planning to get married," my mother said—and, for brief wild seconds, dinner, my father, me, the table, silverware, life, everything exploded up into the air, my father and I seeming to tumble about in midair like Dorothy and Toto in the Oz tornado, his strange mad face peering vaguely at my strange mad face. And then everything settled down again, and he and I had a "serious discussion" in the library. I don't remember much about our talk that night, or rather his talk, except that he seemed so sad. And that he cried. In a way it was all very sweet, gentle (and I was so hugely upset). "You're so young," he kept saying. "But you were young," I'd say, mindful of how many times he'd told me of how at nineteen he'd gone down to London on his own. "But I was thirty-three when I got married," he'd say, but not (as I remember) with any note of triumph. He was very nice that night. I felt we were close, the way I'd hoped we would be, could be. Late at night we walked upstairs. He put his arm around my shoulder. We kissed, I think, and said good night. But the next morning things were not so okay. "It's just too sudden," he said. "Too rushed. You're much too young to get married."

"I'm not too young."

"You're still at college. You don't even have a job."

"I'll get a job."

Then suddenly: "Your mother and I didn't send you to all those schools, St. Paul's, Harvard . . . all those schools, for you to end up driving a truck!" He was red in the face. Angry. "For you to end up as nothing!" I didn't know what he was talking about. Driving a truck? He seemed then very strange. I don't know what I said. I probably said that I was twenty-one years old. My litany. "It's out of the question for now," he said.

I went back to Cambridge in numb despair. I hadn't told Amy much on the telephone. She met me at the station. She was wearing some sort of summer dress. No sleeves. Nice. Bare skin. She looked as if she had been at the beach, Tahiti, the last two days. I felt I had just come from the lions' den. We rode solemnly out of Back Bay in the back seat of a cab. I kept wanting to kiss her. She kept wanting to know what had happened. I was scared to tell her just how badly it had gone. She usually thought of me as very old. Mature. I usually thought of me as very old. Now, the two of us in a taxi. A lot of those well-okay-if-you-want-a-kiss kind of kisses. Nothing very satisfactory. I think I wanted her to make love to me in the taxi. Then I told her what had happened. Something of what had happened. Amy started to cry. I started to cry. "But we can get married anyway," I kept saying. "It won't be any good like that," she said. And then: *"What* will we do?"

We drove in towards Harvard Square. A sunlit afternoon. The red-brick buildings. At Mt. Auburn Street, a traffic light, she jumped out of the cab. Suddenly in tears again. She waved to me not to come after her. I went back to my room. It seemed like a grownup masculine sort of thing to do. I fiddled with things. Opened a beer. Then lunged at the telephone, started calling her. She wasn't in. I went tearing off across the college, across the Square, down all those tranquil side streets, and finally found her sitting calmly on some stone steps out near the building where she lived. We went and got my car, and drove, as we'd often driven before, out towards Ipswich. Ipswich had been where we'd first gone. March. March winds. Still cold. David Kennan's empty house. David Kennan's parents' empty house. Ipswich had been good luck, had been the real spring. We went out there again, drove down Argilla Road. Amy was very silent. There was this restaurant down near the beach. "Do you want to eat?" I asked, nearly gagging over the word "eat." No, she said. We went down on the beach. There were other people there now. Summertime approaching. It felt unfamiliar. A family was having a picnic. We went past them, Amy holding her shoes. I looked along the line of dunes. I was trying to avoid the precise places we'd been to before. It was late afternoon, the sun going down. The sand on the beach was still warm. Everything seemed quite lifeless and frightening. We sat down behind a hillock, out of sight. Amy slightly in front of me. I put my hand on her shoulder. Bare skin. She was looking out at the water. "I always thought your mother was so *nice*," she said, in a kind of bewilderment. "It doesn't matter what my mother thinks," I said. "I don't believe you," she said. "Besides I'm not like that. It matters to me." We talked in low, thin chords. Suddenly I wanted her very much, wanted something, and pulled her around, pulled her to me, kissed her, a very dry kiss from her, I held her hair, her head, and could feel her brain thinking, whirring, kissed her again, some more, could feel her change, the sea change—we made love violently, at least I thought she came to it as violently as I did, but then all of a sudden she was twisting her head and saying no, no, no, but I kept on anyway; there was no love on either of our parts just then, I'd never known that to happen: to have love at stake and then find nothing.

We sat up afterwards. It must have been like a movie. We were both hurt. And playing hurt. A lot of staring at the sea, the mild Ipswich sea, which by then was so dark and black against the night sky that you couldn't make out anything, except the soft swish of waves. And hands placed on hands. On arms. Elbows. Thighs. My hand on her arm, but the nerve ends in the hand, as well as in the arm, now each seemingly turned inward. She was nineteen at the time. She had blue eyes. Brown hair. Wore neutral lipstick. She had had her coming-out party two years before at the Far Hills Country Club. She was writing her term paper for Mark Schorer on "sexual symbolism" in the Malabar Caves, which I thought very exciting. Everything was terrible. "I want to marry you," she said. And then: "I can't marry you." It went on like that for most of the two weeks before the end of college. We'd scrape at each other, rub each other raw, clasp, unclasp, take hungry nighttime rides off in the country, endure the ritual of movies, of little dinners at little Cambridge French restaurants. One evening she said that her mother was planning to take her on a trip to Canada that summer. But you can't go, I said. She looked confused, defensive. How can I get out of it? Tell her you don't want to go, I said. But how? she asked. *How* can I get out of it? I don't know, I said. I wrote my mother to stop sending me my allowance. I was old enough to be on my own, I said. I was old enough to be married. My allowance arrived a few days later in the mail. Amy wouldn't come back with me any more to my room off Henry Street. It didn't seem right, she said. We'd walk instead. We must have walked a couple of thousand miles in those late evenings, the air warm, sweet, leafy, the trees now full of leaves, the feeling of end-of-term in the air; boys and girls (they seemed like boys and girls) gliding cheerfully by in the streets, bicycles, book bags, books, exams. We were taking exams too, although I don't remember much about that. I did okay in history, but not so well in Greek, and nearly failed Proust-Joyce-and-Mann, which gave me a dull scare. Amy did fine. Schorer gave her an A, and asked her to tea. "He's a really nice man," she said. I nodded yes. We'd sit on a lot of fences. Walls. And stand. And walk and walk. "Maybe your parents are right," she'd say.

"They're not right," I said. "Maybe we should wait," she'd say. "There's no point in waiting," I said. "Where will we live?" I used to carry my jacket over my shoulder. "In New York," I said. "Then maybe Europe."

"Oh, where in Europe?"

"Paris," I said. Paris seemed a nice place.

"Oh, I'd love to live in Paris," she said. Suddenly happy. Delirious. Laughter. We'd kiss. Kiss more. "Come home with me."

"No." Then: "Yes." Then: "How will we live?"

"I'll get a job. Come home with me."

"What job?"

"Oh, I'll get a job." Angry. Trees overhead. People walking by us on the sidewalk.

"I don't know," she said. And: "Maybe they're right." And: "Please. Oh *please*. Think of something."

A few mornings later. A lovely morning. I was sitting beside the Charles on that strip of lawn in front of Eliot House. The grass was warm, had just been cut. There were some scullers on the river. I was sitting out there with Douglas. We were supposedly studying. For the last exam. Some friends came by. Most of them younger, most of them staying on at college. A couple of girls were with them, girly-girls who went to a school out near Dedham. A boy called Harris was going on about the problem of getting out the next issue of the magazine.

He had on khaki trousers, a blue button-down shirt, sneakers, and sat beside us on the grass, talking about cartoons and freshman candidates. There was talk of parties. Bashes. Somebody asked about this boat that Henderson had chartered to take everybody down to the Yale-Harvard races. Was I going on this boat that Henderson had chartered to take everybody down to the Yale-Harvard races? The air seemed very warm and liquid. Somebody said he was about to flunk Elder's course. George was going to finish his story by the weekend. George wasn't going to do the editorial. We'd have to find somebody else to do the editorial. I suddenly couldn't stand being at college another moment, all those endless, seemingly endless years of academies, institutions, schools, games, baseball, football, cricket, soccer, masters, teachers, rectors, deans, Yale-Harvard, khaki slacks, parties, bashes, Henderson and his lunatic cherubic face. The lovely red-brick buildings. The lovely scullers upon the lovely river. I tried to reach Amy on the telephone, couldn't. Alone in my room that afternoon, not really having planned out anything at all, I picked up the phone and called a man I knew, a man I'd briefly met, David Palmer, who worked on *Life*. He was an Editor. An Associate Editor. Thirty years old. He'd been at Harvard before the war, now edited the Nature Department. I said simply that I wanted a job. "I thought you were going to Cambridge," he said, which had been one of my vague studious plans, the last time we'd met, that I go and take a year of modern history or something in England. "That's changed," I said. "I'm going to get married. I need a job." He was very nice to me on the phone, he wished me well about "the girl" (in his formality making the whole thing sound more real to me than it had felt in weeks), and said when would I like to come down. I said "right away" and he was nice about that too, he said he'd set something up for me with "Mr. Bermingham." I went on down the next morning. I didn't tell my parents about it, went right down to Time-Life, up up in that elevator. My new brown J. Press suit. The hair well-combed. Mr. Bermingham sat behind a large desk, a small soft-spoken man. I sat on the edge of my chair, as usual, clutching a manila folder full of bits of college magazines and tearsheets. He started to interview me. He would begin each sentence, most of which had something to do with "picture journalism," floating the first part out to me across the desk, then swiveling as he spoke, swiveling slowly in his chair, so that the end of the sentence, most of it in fact, was wafted out the window, out into the spaces of Rockefeller Center. It was like a guessing game. I was so serious. I felt everything was at stake. I spoke with what must have seemed to him a quite lunatic enthusiasm for "picture journalism." For "group journalism." I thrust my manila folder across his desk. He accepted it calmly. He said he'd "be in touch." I went back to Cambridge that evening. Amy was studying for her last exam. I told her what I'd done. "Oh, I *know* they'll take you," she said. "I know, I know." I didn't think so myself. But two days later I received a message to call Mr. Bermingham in New York, and called him, and he said when can you start. Right now, I said. I phoned my parents, my mother in fact, and told her I now had a job and so would not be at graduation. "A summer job?" she asked. "A job," I said. "A real job." I felt truly excited, pleased. "I need money to get married," I said. "Oh," she said. "You're still thinking of that, are you?" But I didn't pay her too much heed that evening. Later my father phoned me, pleased at the job, it's a good company, he said stolidly. Harry Luce and I don't always agree on things, but it's a good company. I hear they give you plenty of time to write on your own. He was clearly worried, though, that I would not get my diploma if I failed to attend graduation. They mail it to you, I explained. Which was true. He seemed doubtful. I think he had imagined something with a bit more organ music. Ceremony. Choirs of angels. "It doesn't sound right to me," he said.

I started work at *Life*. Amy came down from college. I'd spend my days shuffling through wire-service photographs, neat little piles of UP, AP, INS, and then at six in the evening, trying not to show unseemly haste, but obviously showing it, would tear off uptown to Amy's place, or, more precisely, to Amy's mother's place. Amy's mother was drinking champagne that summer. The refrigerator was always full of the stuff. I thought Amy's mother was very sophisticated and intellectual. She read Yeats. She had known Sherwood Anderson "personally." That summer, *Life* was in the process of publishing Hemingway's *The Old Man and the Sea* and I'd bring galleys home with me—an indication, which I hoped everyone would find reassuring, of how far I had proceeded into the professional world. Galleys! We drank champagne. We had literary discussions *à trois*. One evening, Amy announced that indeed she and her mother were going off to Canada. "But how *can* you still?" I was stunned. "Mummy thinks I should have a rest."

"You don't need a rest," I said. "What do *you* think?"

"I don't know," she said.

"Don't go," I said. "We're going to get married." I started to cry. I must have spent that entire summer alternately sweating and crying.

"Nobody approves," Amy said. Patient. Explaining to a child.

"But why does everyone have to approve? We can just get married. We can get a room somewhere." I was very big on getting a room somewhere, it seemed like such a nice idea. Amy began to cry. Her mother appeared from downstairs. "Aren't you two going to have any dinner?" she'd ask. "We're not hungry," Amy said. Her mother sat down on the big sofa. Amy on the far end of it. I now on a chair opposite. We would have another literary discussion. Champagne. The time that Sherwood came to the house that summer . . . More champagne. Eventually, she'd stir her feet a little, say, Well I think I'll go to bed and read for a while . . . Then a bit more champagne. The time that Heywood Broun was glimpsed in Madison, Conn., that autumn . . . I'd try to catch Amy's eye, make some sort of conspiratorial sign. Amy, the dutiful daughter. Prim hands. Legs tucked under her. At last, her mother standing upright. Her mother moving forward. Her mother, great admirer of the poets, friend of Sherwood Anderson, glimpser of Broun, trudging off to slumberland with the new Ellery Queen clutched in her hand. The sound of the bedroom door opening. The bedroom door closing. I'd dive for Amy. "No!" she'd say. "Not yet. She can still hear." The Irish serving girl caught between-stairs by the uncouth laird. Oh those inelegances, the big blue sofa, the rumpled clothes, the back-seat-of-the-car fifteen floors above Park Avenue. "Don't leave," she'd say. "Please leave. Don't leave." It sounds good in stories but it was nerve-racking in life. One had those rubber things then, awful things in trim little tinfoily packages. Amy saying yes and no. White legs against the blue sofa. Yes and No. Just a moment, Amy. Wait. Yes and No. The little package in one's hands. One's body suddenly feeling stupid. For a time, I tried putting the damn things on beforehand—standing upright in the bathroom at the cocktail hour, the sound of champagne glasses in the living room, her mother trilling on about something, my fly unzipped, tugging on this wretched rubber, pushing, pulling. Soft rubber. Limp flesh. The whole thing ridiculous, and doomed. Once, coming out of the bathroom after much flushing of toilets, walking debonairly, airily back into the living room, I could feel the damned thing slipping off, slipping, slipping, I could feel it fall down inside my trousers. I stopped. Tried to keep looking straight ahead, felt around with my foot. "Whatever are you staring at?" her mother said. "What a funny expression."

A few hours after such an evening, such a morning, Amy and her mother left for Canada. For two weeks. I thought I would use the time to remain more at home. To be with my parents. I thought this would be nice for them. After dinner, my father and mother would be reading in the library. "What do you hear from Amy?" my mother would ask. I had heard nothing. "Nothing," I said. Besides, I resented the question. "I imagine she's having a nice time," she'd say. "I guess so," I'd reply. My mother would pick up her Daphne du Maurier. "Well, I imagine she probably appreciates a little time to think things over." In seconds I'd be out of my chair. Smoke. Fire. "She is *not* thinking things over!" I'd say. "I am not a child!"

"You're both children," my mother would say.

I'd glower at my father. He pretended to be reading. "I'm going out," I'd say. I had some friends at *Life* who lived in an old building down on Fifty-third Street. The men were very lean and tall and hard-working and sincere. I admired them hugely. The girls were okay, soft, matter-of-fact. Pleasant. It was all very professional. We drank whisky, and talked about assignments and stories and editors, and how all of us would do things better. It was nice. And nobody cried. I could spend whole evenings with these people and none of them would suddenly break into tears, I wouldn't break into tears. The world seemed rational. I laughed. Made jokes. The feel of hard ground underfoot. Sometimes walking home late at night, I had these mad rushes of desire for Amy. But in the morning, waking up, thinking of her, she had no face. I tried to remember her face. The week was odd that way. Then one day the office boy brought me a letter, the postmark Canada, the address in her handwriting, a script that made a brave but not very successful attempt to escape the Farmington curlicues. I dreaded it suddenly, put it down. Didn't want to open it. Opened it, read. She was miserable, lonely. She was coming back. I felt very strange. And then she did come back. "We have to do something," she said. The edge of her elation, like mine, was fierce, but very thin. She seemed unhappy. I didn't know what I was. "We'll get married," I said. "But how can we?" she said. "We don't need everybody's approval," I said. "I'm not a child. I'm twenty-one. I have a job."

"I'm nineteen," she said.

"I know. Your mother will approve."

"I'm not so sure she will any more," she said.

I went to lunch with my father. You look miserable, he said. I'm not miserable, I said. Do you really want to get married now, he said. Of course I want to get married now. Suppose you have children, he said. I want children, I said. We talked like that, and then walked uptown staring at shop windows. My mother seemed close to rage all the time. "That wretched little Mrs. Wells!" she finally flung out at me, about nothing really. I'd just mentioned her name. "What do you mean?" I said. I knew what she meant. I couldn't bear that she would think it, say it. I went with Amy to visit friends of hers in Connecticut. A big ample cozy house. The friends were married. Everything there seemed so firm, stable, nailed down. I loved it all, desired it. I sat alone with Amy before dinner in the big living room. Maple furniture. Abercrombie & Fitch ashtrays. I put my hand between her legs. It was very quiet. Peaceful. Later, everyone asleep, she would not make love. We wandered around fields drearily the next day. Back in town on Monday. "I love you," I said. "I love you," she said. We stood outside of Schrafft's at Seventy-ninth Street. "Let's go away," I said. "Where?" she said. Doubtful. "It doesn't matter where," I said. "It matters," she said. Once again at home my mother asked me if she were pregnant. I screamed back No. Amy said she thought her mother would let her get engaged. She talked of parties. She would have an engagement party. She drew up lists. She said her mother was fond of me. She said her mother considered my father a very sophisticated writer. One day she met me after work. Standing down by the elevators. Her face white. Drawn. She said her mother had told her she should go back to college. I don't know what to do, she said. *Do* something. She wouldn't make love any more. She was afraid about having children, she said. But if we're going to be married . . . I said. I want things to be right, she said. I then determined, decided, that we should be married. I rented an apartment, over on East Eighty-eighth Street. Unfurnished. Two rooms. I ordered a bed from Bloomingdale's and called them nine times a day to assure that it be delivered instantly, at least within the next two weeks. I began to be very scared, I didn't know of what. I began to have great tearing crying fights with my mother—the library late at night, hot tears, indignation. "I don't care what you think," I said.

And: "It's my life." And: "You don't understand."
My mother on her tenth drink, her voice very deep.
My father asleep upstairs, or trying to be asleep. "If
she loves you that much," my mother said, "she'll
marry you whether I approve or not."

And then I began to hear Amy's voice, as if I
hadn't been hearing it for months and months,
had been hearing something else, something she'd
briefly become. One fall evening, I remember, we'd
gone to a party. A dance out in the country somewhere. Long Island. Some friends of my sister's
were giving it. On the way there, we talked, Amy
and I. Chatter. About how much too old we felt for
this sort of thing. Lester Lanin. "Just One of Those
Things." Those elbow-wiggling little schoolboy
dances. I now had all these new friends at *Life*. Professional people. We drank whisky together and
talked about careers. At the party, Amy looked very
pretty. I danced with her a lot at first. I really wasn't
much interested in most of the people there. And
then later, walking into one of the smaller rooms by
myself, I saw her over by the piano. Somebody was
playing the piano. She was with a group—boys, girls,
young men I vaguely recognized, whom she'd known
before we met. Yale. Far Hills. She was standing beside the piano, keeping time to the music with her
head, her shoulders. She seemed so light. Sexy.
Young-sexy. Carefree. I felt this great pang and
thought at first it must be jealousy. I must be jeal-

ous of Dick Thomas or Ned Somebody. But no, I knew I wasn't jealous of Dick or Ned. And then, still moving her head, her body, a kind of private dance, she turned, saw me, and oh God the sudden gravity—the start, and then the gravity seeping back into those eyes. And then it left, and something more operable replaced it. I wanted to say, no, *please*. But I knew it was true, something had been true then. Something had been true in that surprised look. I really loved her very much just then, more than I had loved her in months and months, since Ipswich in March maybe, and dancing on the windy beach, which was the first time I had been in love with anybody. And I knew what it all meant, too, about the shoulders bobbing to the music, and Dick, and Ned, and the engagement party lists, and the gray-silk dress she wore, which she had worn two summers ago to her own coming-out party—I knew at least enough just then to say you love me but you don't love me that much, nor do I probably love you that much, and neither of us should have to. I knew enough to say that, but I didn't. I wanted her. Or something. I never ever told her any of that, which I think was true.

It was September then. And afterwards October. Early October. I remember very well the time. The air now clear and turning cool. A time of year I'd always loved, a time of birth—and hated then. She was wearing a new coat. Black. A small fur collar.

Her face very white. Tense, washed out. She seemed the grownup one just at that moment. My mother says I have to go back to college, she said. I heard her, heard the words, had heard them before. It seemed like such a procedural consideration. I said, But you can go back to college later. If you don't want to go back now, you don't have to. We were standing outside her building. Close by the wall. "I don't know any more," she said. "I love you," I said. I looked at her. There was by now this great thick screen between us. "You should have *made* it right!" she suddenly cried. "You love me," I said. "You should have *made* me marry you!" she screamed. And broke into tears. And ran inside. Her mother called me the next day at the office to say that she was taking Amy "to the South" that afternoon. Amy left, and then she came back briefly. A brief pale ghost. And then she and her mother went to San Francisco for the year, and I was in the Army.

I'VE OFTEN WONDERED HOW MY MOTH-
er and father were together in bed. Have wondered
lately, I should say, because at first I didn't think
about it at all, except secretly, that sudden wild
thought, the image of two people on the bed, forcing
itself almost physically into the side edge of one's
mind, exploding briefly, and then gone. And later,
still not thinking about it very much, I more or less
assumed that they were very good. Whatever that
meant. They loved each other a lot. They kept telling each other that they loved each other a lot. They
told me that they loved each other a lot. Oh, I knew
they had their arguments, their temperamental differences. They would display their disagreements

sometimes, almost as an act, the sort of act a well-teamed husband and wife might perform publicly together. Look now, we have these differences. In actuality, they had few fights. Doubtless they had some in private, or I would hope so anyway. But I guess one learns that if husbands and wives fight much in private, sooner or later they fight in public, or at any rate "before the children," and there wasn't ever much of that. My mother seemed affectionate and deferential towards my father. My father seemed adoring and considerate towards her. Friends would often compliment them on their marriage. I see them together of a certain evening. The library. Curtains drawn. A guest is there, talking to my father. The guest is English, togged up in one of those steel-thick suits. He is enjoying, he keeps saying, one of his "last days of civilization" before setting off on a lecture tour of South Dakota. My father sits in the green chair. Gray trousers. Beige Sulka shirt, silky, open at the neck. An ascot around the neck. A brown-checked, loose-hanging jacket. There is a rustling in the hall. My mother comes into the room. Long flowing gown. Dark hair, now very gray, piled high, swept high atop her head. She smiles. Gives her hand. My father and the visitor are standing. My father brings her a drink. She settles down into the couch. "Jocelyn was just telling us about . . ." my father says. Conversation. It is all so lovely. It is a ballet. The little glasses in everyone's hand. The room so quiet, private, enfolding. The visitor makes more jokes about South Dakota. Another drink. The maid comes in to pass around bits of things upon a platter. "How simply marvelous," the visitor says. After a bit he leaves. We all have dinner, and then I go out, and then they have coffee in the library, read. Read. Drink. My mother drinks a lot, I know. At first I don't notice it, try not to. At first, long ago, I'd rather liked it—back in those first years in New York, coming down from school on holidays, I used to make her drinks. Old-Fashioneds they were then. Sugar. Bitters. Slice of orange. I never got it quite right about the bitters. Now it is mostly Scotch. Scotch and soda. Before dinner in a short glass. After dinner in a tall glass. Most evenings now she stays up very late, long after my father has gone to bed. "It's a good thing I always nurse my drinks," she says. One whole evening I watch her. Like a spy. Awful. She drinks a great deal in those days. Sometimes she erupts in sudden black rages. America. The Bloomingdale's credit department. Me. General Eisenhower. My father paces alone all afternoon inside that library. And all the while, this adoration . . . *dearest* . . . *my beauty* . . . *beautiful*. My father is so gentle towards her, in his ways of telling her she is beautiful. He tells *me* she is beautiful. Your mother is a very beautiful woman, things like that. (My mother, what the hell. Annabelle French, who lived on the third floor, was beautiful. But still I know . . .) Gentleness. Consideration. Love. I have some of that in me, now grown, this gentleness, and much of it is false—false gentleness—and so I wonder how much of that was in him. Another speculation, unanswerable. But sometimes I read his books again, look into them, catch momentary, almost thrown-aside flashes of him from inside his writing. Real flashes. The flash of how he looked at times. Alone. With other people. I wonder (one of the many things I wonder) how all that nerve and passion got so locked in, allowed itself to go underground. Fear? One talks so facilely of fear these days. Indeed he must have been fearful of so much, and how I can imagine him detesting that sentence, and how I can imagine the people who knew him reading that and becoming angry. Fear? Why, he had all the nerve in the world. Do you not remember how he first came on to London? Do you not remember how he won your mother? Do you not remember that time when Goebbels was staying at the Imperial, on the floor below, and stepped onto his balcony, and your father went to the sideboard, mixed a Martini, very exquisitely called down to Goebbels, and poured it on his upturned face? Do you not remember? I think I do, or partly so anyway. I remember a lot, because the two of them, this man and woman, were vividly drawn, and in the foreground, and I paid (it seems) attention more to figures than to landscape. Still I wonder about them in bed, because although "bed" doesn't tell you everything about anybody, what it does tell seems true to itself, inescapably true to itself; and maybe the history on many people's faces has at least a good deal to do with trying to escape what is told at night, in those odd moments. I think sometimes of my father when he was young (and out of sight to me). I try to imagine how he must have been—the afternoon he first heard from Heinemann's of their enthusiasm for *The Green Hat*. (He told me that on his way back home he stopped in at Cartier and bought himself a jeweled stickpin; my mother gave it to me after his death, a little duck, blue and white on gold; a jaunty thing.) And later. All the photographs. They were a very striking pair. Much love. There are all these photographs remaining, often of the two of them looking at each other. I really wonder what they saw. The other night I brought some of them out, laid them on the floor. I was looking for one for this book. It is quite haunting to look at photographs of any two people, young, *connected,* beginning one of those mythic, meshed, knowing, unknowing journeys. Austria. Golf at Antibes. In-front-of-the-Savoy. I thought of him, his family, spinning, whirling, spinning away from them (the old lady in rimless glasses in the room in Lancashire), the ambition, driving forward, momentum, momentum, success, reaching out now for all the shiny things he'd dreamed about, *reaching* (and now the woman beside him, the marvelous woman, golf at Antibes), catching—catching what? Warmth? Beauty? Children in English clothes? Sometimes (one guesses) the air must have been as stifling as death. And she, the girl in the new golfing jacket, quiet-looking, beautiful, hanging back a little in the picture, a slightly "foreign" look, a not quite gentle smile, the girl who worried over what to say to Mr. Maugham, or what to write in a thank-you note to Lady Mendl, who embraced her children (sometimes) like a peasant, who surely needed (those deep eyes) more than being made love to, or wrapped in endearments and adorations, to be fucked—there is no other word now, is there? What of her? Golf at Antibes. Death. Things in between. I picked up the photographs and stashed them away. There is a place I keep them in the basement, an old suitcase.

$\mathcal{A}$SHBURY COLLEGE: THE FACT THAT they called it a college when it so obviously wasn't seemed typical of the place, although I shortly learned that a number of the other private schools in Canada called themselves colleges—a wishful note of dignity, I guess. Ashbury consisted of one main red-brick building. Three stories tall. Gabled. Dark red brick, much more ominous and Victorian and English than anything I'd seen in England. The building was T-shaped, with the dormitory rooms in front, then classrooms along a narrow corridor, then out in back a gym of sorts, and outside the playing fields. The whole thing enclosed in a perimeter of Cyclone fence, although whether to keep the heathen out, or the young gentlemen in, was never clear. Also

another small building off to the side, white clapboard with a green roof. The headmaster's house.
The headmaster then, the "head," was a man called
Faircloth, Andrew Faircloth, an athletic Canadian,
probably in his mid-forties, with a cheery pale angular
face, thinning blond hair, also a large stern wife,
and three daughters whom he kept as far away from
the school as possible, except on Sundays, when they
all sidled into church together. Three blond girls in
gray uniforms. One of them was pretty, too. "Onward Christian Soldiers" was Mr. Faircloth's favorite
hymn, and we sang it fairly often there in Sunday
chapel, standing upright in the wooden pews, bel-
lowing out the warlike phrases, sunlight coming in
the stained-glass windows (which had not been fully
stained as yet, owing to a deficit in the stained-
glass-window fund), thinking the usual thoughts
about sports or what to do the rest of the day, or
directing imprecise covetous glances at Polly Faircloth.

Ashbury was a school originally intended for
about one hundred and fifty of the sons of the more
prosperous Ottawa businessmen, and now, by virtue
of the bonds of Commonwealth, and maybe of yearn-
ing for a little more tuition, contained an additional
hundred or so of us evacuees from Abinger in
England, most of us younger than the Canadians,
smaller, still wandering around, that first autumn,
in our English schoolboy uniforms of brown blazers,

brown shorts, those little peaked caps. Rooms, lino-
leum corridors lined with rooms. Five beds to a
room, where usually two or three had been before.
A metal bed. A chair beside the bed. A washbasin
inside the room. One hung one's towel and wash-
cloth over the metal bar at the foot of the bed. Bedroom slippers were to be placed beneath the chair.
Cake of soap on top of the chair. My mother sent
me clothes up from New York, that faraway place
I'd not yet been to. More shorts. "None of the boys
wear shorts any more here, except the Abinger boys,
who don't have anything else," I wrote. Some long
trousers arrived, my first long trousers—corduroys,
as thick as buffalo hide. "I have asked Rogers Peet
to send you up some trousers," my mother had
written, "but naturally, since you refuse to send me
your proper measurements, as to outside seam, inside
seam, etc., they certainly will not fit. I ordered corduroy since the material is durable and will last
longer."

Everything was very strange at first at Ashbury,
and dreary. That dour red-brick building. The classrooms with their smell of chalk, and ink, and little
copybooks. The gray cold streets of suburban Ottawa
outside. On Saturday afternoons we were allowed to
go outside the fence. Right after lunch, one lined up
in the corridor outside Mr. Marsden's office, and
waited in turn, and stepped inside, and called one's
name, and Mr. Marsden dipped into a petty-cash

box and handed one twenty-five cents' allowance. With twenty-five cents one could do one of two things: one could walk with it out the gates, and down the hill a mile towards Rockcliffe, where there was a sort of glop-and-candy store, and buy some glop, usually a huge bottle of soda and some squishy cakes, and take it back to school; or one could sweat out the need for glop and candy that particular Saturday, stay at school, kick soccer balls around the empty fields, and then next weekend, armed with fifty cents, one could take the streetcar into Ottawa for ten cents, see a movie for twenty cents, and then come back out again in time for dinner.

That first fall I shared a room with a boy called George Sargent, who had been at Abinger with me, a nice boy, about my age, ten, tousled blond hair, fair skin (very fast and scrappy on the soccer field); he'd grown up in Yorkshire, where his father had a small livestock farm. His young brother had come over with him, Nicholas, a roly-poly little English boy, no more than eight. He was in with us too, a room at the end of one of the corridors, the three of us, and two Canadian boys. It was all in a way very friendly, and lonely. I remember Nicholas crying a good deal, especially at night, and George telling him crossly to "be a man." George and I practiced soccer maneuvers together after the regular practice was over. Corner kicks. George was going to go back to England and be a great left-wing for

Yorkshire. One morning, I remember, they called him out of class and told him, I think it was Mr. Faircloth who told him, that his father, who was in the R.A.F., had been killed. For days and days he didn't say a word, didn't speak, cry, anything. He had told Mr. Faircloth that he would be the one to tell Nicholas, no one else. Each evening, George would sit on his bed—he had a model airplane he was building, and he would lay all the pieces out, precise little slivers of balsa wood, and glue, and sit cross-legged on the olive-colored blanket, and arrange and rearrange the pieces, and now and then take up the knife and cut a little slit in one of them, and fit two together. Then one evening he began to cry. Nicholas sitting at the foot of the bed, as he usually did. George holding pieces of his model airplane, tears trickling down his face. Nicholas didn't know what to do. I remember George then holding Nicholas, all I can really remember is how Nicholas seemed, the back of Nicholas's head, curly hair, and Nicholas at one point saying, "But was it really a Spitfire?" (which had been the plane their father flew), and George just holding Nicholas, eyes so tightly clenched, that English thing of fighting back the tears, nodding his head. All that time my mother wrote me letters. I wrote her letters back. I looked at some of them the other day, my mother saved everything. "Dear Mummy, I am glad to hear that you are well. The Latin is going well. Mr. Marsden

says it is the equal of first year at Eton. I am trying
out for right wing at soccer. Jonathan H. plays in-
side-right but I think they are going to move him
back to half because he is slow. Well I think I had
better run. Love . . ." And then one day, one weekend, later that year, she came up to visit me. We
walked around the school. Mr. Faircloth showed her
the hockey rink. Mr. Marsden showed her the in-
firmary. She was staying in Ottawa, at the Château
Laurier, a big hotel opposite the railroad station. I
thought the Château Laurier very grand, it was not
a side of Ottawa life I'd been much exposed to. I
went in there with her the afternoon she was to go
back to New York. She had her suitcase open on
the bed, a number of books beside it. She'd brought
up all these books for me, books about trains, books
about animals, books about fish—I remember especially the book about fish, *Wild Game Fish* I think
it was. I could still almost remember back in Cannes
when she'd sat on my bed, when I had measles or
something, and had drawn pictures of animals with
me, for me, and now, reaching out, reaching out
doubtless of her own limbo for something to have
connective between us, had reached out and found
a book on fish. I remember thanking her for the
books, sitting on the bed beside her, the books on
my lap, in truth being very pleased. And then we
went down to lunch, it seemed like years since I had
had lunch with her. There was one of those big

overstuffed hotel dining rooms, and we went in there, and for brief seconds it was as everything had always been, the world in place, my mother ordering her drink, the way she lit a cigarette, the rings on her hand. "They must be starving you," she said. And, "You must eat everything you want," and of course I couldn't eat anything, but that was okay. She couldn't either. And then we went upstairs, and I made sure to get the books together, and took the rattly streetcar back to school.

$\mathcal{T}$HE WAY I FINALLY CAME TO GO TO
school in the United States was like this: in my
fourth year at the Canadian school, springtime, sitting at dinner one evening in the big green dining
room, ten long tables, two dozen thirteen-year-olds
all in a row tossing down creamed beef on pieces of
bread, I was handed a telegram from my mother.
My mother usually wasn't much of one for the casual telegram. This one said: "You just accepted St.
Paul's School New Hampshire starting September
letter follows. Love . . ." A letter duly followed a
few days later, four pages of my mother's great slant-
ing thick-nibbed handwriting, and virtually all about
clothes. I should remember to bring all my white
shirts. I should be sure to bring both parts to my

suit. My black shoes. My socks. My head. There was something at the end, about asking Mr. Faircloth to send my "files" (which sounded very sinister) to somebody with a decidedly religious-sounding title at St. Paul's. My mother seemed very sprightly about it all, especially the business about clothes, which was one of those subjects, like packing, which she clearly enjoyed getting hold of, and then swinging around her head like an iron ball on the end of a chain. I wasn't at all sure I wanted to go to St. Paul's. To begin with, I'd never heard of it, and there was some airy reference in my mother's letter to its being a "church school," which conjured up (not entirely unjustified) visions of incense and ecumenical robes and the singing of "Onward Christian Soldiers" twelve times a day. Also, I was beginning to get used to Ashbury. In the past year or so, nearly all the Abinger boys who had come over with me on the boat from England had gone home again, or to other places, and I had begun to settle in at being Canadian in a now all-Canadian school. I cared a lot about the Ottawa Rough Riders, the local football team. I collected bubble-gum cards of famous Canadian hockey players. I was getting to know Ottawa as though I lived there, which I suppose I did. And then there was the cricket.

It seems odd to me looking back on it now, something far away and remote that surely must have happened to somebody else, but there was a time when I cared very much about cricket, and got to be quite good at it. I started in England—I started actually in France, my father lobbing cricket balls at me to catch (it never occurred to me until this moment to think of my father as a sort of expatriate Little League parent). But in England, at my first school, I realized that there was at least one genuine certifiable 100 percent *English* thing I could do reasonably well, which was to catch a cricket ball; and so made the best of it, going out into the fields after those high teas we used to have, late afternoon, evening, until the twilight finally made it impossible to see the ball, taking turns with some amenable friend at batting balls up into the air, standing under them, dizzy, afraid, the red ball against the sky, the red ball very hard, bare hands, very hard.

There was a history master at Abinger called Sykes, who had allegedly "played for Kent," quite an honor if true, and it probably was (he wasn't much at history anyway), a great muscular left-hander, an immense left arm. He was a bowler, I wanted to be a bowler, and he came with the school over to Canada, where he taught Cromwell and the Long Parliament in a fine county accent in the morning, and cricket to us and the Canadians in the afternoon. The Canadians were very keen on cricket then, I suppose it was the colonial thing, but in any case it was the big spring sport at all the schools. The R.C.A.F. had a team. The Canadian Navy had a team. I used to watch every match I could, and would at times sneak out of study hall to watch the Ashbury "first eleven" practice, those great eighteen-year-old giants in their white shirts, white flannels, long white flannels, the little caps—the "nets," where the batter stood at one end, the bowler at the other, Sykes standing by, smoking a pipe, some ancient faded English university blazer around his shoulders. "You don't need all that run!" he'd say, the universal coach's strange mixture of impatience, diffidence, worry, the desire to somehow lay little tongues of fire upon the unanointed. "Use the shoulder more! Get the weight right—" And then sometimes Sykes himself (he couldn't have been much over thirty) would take up the ball, and measure off his paces behind the bowling wicket—I can still see that great left arm dangling, freaklike, wonderful—and start his run, a fairly short run, almost a lope, then suddenly the slight turn sideways, the arm coming way around, the whole body pitched forward—Sykes really threw a very fast ball, with lots of control. I thought it marvelous, bowling marvelous (him marvelous), and practiced for hours, usually by myself on weekends, there not being much else to do, or with such companions as one could find, or sometimes on Sunday afternoons with Sykes himself, who didn't seem to have much to do either.

Then one day Sykes told me I should meet him at such-and-such hour the next Sunday morning in

front of the school, and be sure to wear your best
flannels, he said, and do you have a clean shirt, he
said, and get your shoes in shape, he said. I couldn't
tell what was happening, spent the whole night before arranging and rearranging my clothes, putting
that white gunk on my shoes, sitting down, lying
down, getting up. I met Sykes at the appointed time.
He was standing in front of the school, leaning on
his bicycle—long white trousers, a very splendid
blazer, and a little peaked cap with all sorts of gor-
geous colors. "Now get your bicycle," he said. And
we rode off, Sykes still not saying much of anything,
a mile or so down side roads where I hadn't been
before, thick trees, a sort of park, and then we were
at the gates of what I knew was the Governor-
General's estate, guards, policemen, we cycled blithely through, Sykes puffing on his pipe, me pedaling
hard to keep apace with him, great avenues of elm
and maple, expanses of lawn, garden, trimmed
hedges, and then at last a sort of white pavilion,
some few cars, a cricket field, men in white flannels.
We left our bikes beside the pavilion, I followed
Sykes. Some of the men called to him by name. A
large red-faced man, also in white flannels, with a
great walrus mustache, came up to us. He shook
hands fiercely with Sykes. "So this is the boy?" he
said, looking at me. I stood speechless. "Well, shake
hands," said Sykes in a kindly way. "This is Colonel
Knox." I shook hands with Colonel Knox. "We'll

see," he said cryptically, and strode away. Colonel Knox, it turned out, was captain of what was called the Governor-General's Eleven, a very grand (to me) and gentlemanly team of cricketers, who played the R.C.A.F., and Navy, and various university teams (various lesser university teams, I should now imagine); and after that Sunday, in which I played about five minutes, five terror-stricken minutes in an obscure part of the field, one not normally hit to, and made no mistakes (I think I stopped an extremely slow-moving grounder that nobody was running on anyway), I was taken on, obviously as Sykes's protégé, as a sort of utility infielder, a sort of bat boy who now and then got up to bat.

I think those Sundays were up to then the happiest I had been: meeting Sykes in front of the school, cycling down those great shaded avenues on the Governor-General's grounds; and then the whole ritual of the game itself, which must have been so extraordinarily colonial (this was wartime after all) —the Ottawa ladies in their flowing Bournemouth gowns, the men in Old School blazers, the little garden-party lettuce-and-tomato sandwiches passed around on trays between innings. I remember the first thing I thought after getting that telegram from my mother was: would I play cricket at St. Paul's? I imagined probably not, and when I thought about my budding career with the old colonels of the Governor-General's team I felt very sad. I mentioned my forthcoming departure to Sykes, who was going back to England himself that summer. "Don't worry, boy," I remember him saying. "There's always a way and a place to play cricket."

The next Sunday, because of Sykes I think, they let me bowl two innings against a local Army team. I had never been so nervous in my life—can still remember being handed, as is customary, the ball by the umpire, walking off my steps, and then looking down the suddenly unbelievably long pitch towards a gigantic, mustached and bearded Army major, crouched in front of the wickets, making furious little motions with his bat. I didn't get anyone out, but nobody hit me either. "Not bad, not bad," said Sykes later, as we got ready to bicycle home. "I thought you were getting a bit careful with Anderson, but then he was playing it fairly con-serv-ative himself." I rode back to school that afternoon literally exhausted with contentment, Sykes and I pedaling easily down the narrow roads, those two great cricketers, Sykes and Arlen, pedaling back across Ottawa, back across Canada, cheering villages, townspeople, happiness. A few days later, Sykes called me into his study, which as usual was filled with uncorrected exam books, and smelled of the linseed oil he used to oil his cricket bats. "Here," he said, "this may be good news," and handed me an old *Registry of American Schools* opened to an even older engraving of the Worcester Academy cricket eleven, vintage

1896. "I wouldn't be at all surprised," he said, puffing on his pipe, "if some of the solider schools down there still played the game." I must have looked doubtful. Sykes himself suddenly looked doubtful. "Well anyway," he said, "you can always play baseball." He stood up and draped that beautiful overlong left arm over my shoulders. "I hear they play it wearing gloves," he said.

*M*Y MOTHER WENT UP WITH ME TO
St. Paul's that autumn. The night sleeper out of
New York to Boston. The ratty steam-heated little
train out of North Station to Concord, New Hampshire—my mother sitting upright on the faded green
horsehide seat, hair swept high atop her head, a
scarf around the neck, some jewels, one of those
stiffish nineteen-forties suits top-heavy with shoulder
padding and lapels, the Vuitton bottle case open on
the seat beside her. Around us, the coach half full
with soldiers, sailors home on leave. A dozen or so
schoolboys up front, giggling, punching each other
on the arms, passing, puffing, stuffing lighted cigarettes into their mouths like candy. My mother doing
her nails as we chugged past the red-brick mill towns

of New Hampshire. Later, we walked around the school a bit. Green lawns and clapboard buildings. Gardeners, trees, boys in blazers walking in a kind of gentle shuffle down the pathways, it all seemed quite lovely, not like a school at all. We went in to see the man in charge of admissions, a dour, crinkly-faced Scot called Mr. McAndrew. "He'll be in the Second Form," he said, looking at me, "live in the Lower School. We're a bit crowded now. Has he had French?" "Of course he's had French," my mother said. "Has French," Mr. McAndrew repeated, and wrote in pencil on some kind of chart. We went in to see the headmaster, here called the Rector, a stoutish, pink-faced, relentlessly urbane clergyman called Dr. Peavey, who swept around from behind his desk to meet us, more or less transported us into two chairs placed opposite it, offered my mother a cigarette from a gold cigarette case, settled back into his own chair, beamed, rang a little bell—a woman in a maid's uniform appeared. "Tea?" the Rector said. A great paraphernalia of teacups, teapots, cakes, biscuits, spoons and so forth was brought in. The Rector said that he was sorry my father could not be with us. He was still in England, my mother said. The Rector said that all of us would remember the Battle of Britain. The Rector said that London was his favorite city. He and my mother talked about London for a while, my mother sitting attentively, legs crossed, almost shy, smoking a cigarette, declining cakes; the Rector, hands clasped in front of him, prefacing each sentence with "As you doubtless know," "As you certainly are familiar with . . ." Then they talked about me for a while, mostly in the third person. "He's had quite a varied education, hasn't he?" the Rector would say. Or, "I'm sure he'll get along very nicely here . . ." and then beam in my direction as if to show how nicely I was getting along already. "He's been doing a lot of Latin and Greek," I heard my mother say at one point. "Is that so?" the Rector said cheerily. "Well, we have an excellent classics program here." He peered over at me. Tortoise-shell glasses. Clerical collar. His entire shirtfront seemingly crisscrossed with chains and medals and little gold keys. "There's no training like the classics, now, is there?" I nodded dumbly. "We were hoping that he might be able to start in at his own level," my mother continued, in her best between-us-two-professionals tone. "You see, he is quite advanced . . ." The Rector directed another smile at me, this one equal parts radiance and wariness. "Quite *advanced?*" he murmured. I tried to become invisible on my chair. "I'm certain," he said briskly, "that he will find the work here fairly challenging." We shook hands all around. "A great, great pleasure," he said to my mother, placing a fatherly hand over my shoulder. Then a smart clap on the back. "Well, well, young man! 'Arma virumque cano'!" He shook hands again with my mother. "I make it

a point to re-read a little of the poets every summer,"
he said, and ushered us out the door. "Really quite
a civilized man," my mother said thoughtfully, as we
walked over to the Lower School. The dormitory
there already seemed to be filling up with boys,
occasional parents in hats and raincoats lugging in
suitcases. I was assigned a little cubicle, one of fourteen cubicles along one side of a long room, a bed,
a dresser, a chair, a curtain across the front. My
mother sat on the bed while I unpacked my suitcase. "It seems very nice," she said. I agreed. It
seemed in fact quite elegant compared to Ashbury.
A young master came by, stuck his head in. "I only
sent him up with six white shirts," my mother said.
The master looked bewildered. "Oh yes," he said.
"That's fine. White shirts." I wished my mother
would leave. I wished she would never leave. "I
hope you'll work hard now," she said. And, "I know
you'll make friends quickly." And, "Be sure to write
soon." She fished into her handbag and produced a
ten-dollar bill and gave it to me. "I don't know if
they'll let you spend this," she said, "but I'm sure it
will come in handy." I helped her on with her coat,
and we walked down the corridor, past the other
cubicles. Boys' voices. Laughter. A football bouncing
down the floor. A deeply tanned young boy came
slowly in, followed by a woman in a large hat, and
a chauffeur carrying what seemed to be a fishing rod.
The chauffeur climbed on top of a radiator and tried

to shove the fishing rod over one of the cubicles. The boy and I stood off to one side, trying not to look at each other. My mother and I stood on a brick walk outside the dormitory, beside the line of yellow taxis waiting to take away the parents. She kissed me fondly. "You're a good boy, I know you'll do well here," she said. "Be sure to write," she said, and got into the cab, and waved, and blew a kiss.

$\mathcal{A}$ WINTER'S EVENING IN NEW YORK,
946: We live in the Hotel Volney, an apartment-
otel on Seventy-fourth Street, just off Madison.
ray limestone front. A green awning above the
dewalk. The doorman is Irish: Fred, who sits on
 chair just inside the lobby and shuffles to a half-
sing position whenever anyone comes in or leaves.
ew people seem to do either. The lobby is dark,
ak-paneled. The elevator man is also Irish: James,
ick chest and one of those wide seminarian necks,
ale bloodless face, glasses. He follows the horses in
e evening *Sun,* although he says he does not bet.
t night, the front desk is empty, save for Miss Ras-
ussen, a Swede, who sits by the switchboard, and
nokes, and reads movie-star magazines. At the far

155

end of the lobby, beyond the switchboard, there
a dining room. Also dark, oak-paneled. Glass door
A large round table near the entrance covered wit
a display of fruit and pastries which never seems
be changed, or moved, or eaten, or touched, or
have any acknowledged existence at all, except po
sibly as a kind of warning to diners. Tonight,
usual, there are few diners. Mr. Binton, the manag
of the hotel, a tall, dapper and morose gentlema
in his late thirties, sits at his accustomed table again
the far wall. Mr. Binton has been manager of th
Volney for nearly a year, something of a record
managers of the Volney seeming to come and go li
South American dictatorships. Mr. Binton has ve
chops every evening, and reads the paper. Close t
Mr. Binton there is a table with two elderly ladie
The two ladies are what is called "permanent res
dents," wear strange long dresses, are very quiet, a
sometimes have the startled look of sole survivo
from some unimaginably far-off shipwreck, who f
unknown reasons have been washed ashore to d
in the Hotel Volney, most probably in the Hot
Volney dining room. There is also a small tab
containing Dr. Hesseltine, who is an oculist, ve
gaunt (also a "permanent resident"), who wears thi
glasses, and reads a magazine. Also a larger table
the middle of the room, the empty middle, whi
contains two men and two women, evidently hu
bands and wives, quite dressed up too, little hats

e women, small bursts of laughter—a decided air
f the tourist about them. One imagines them having
rayed into this oak-paneled catacomb by mistake,
erhaps lured in by the elegant placard displayed on
e sidewalk in front of the hotel: *The Volney Res-
aurant. Guests Welcome!* The solitary waiter, Gio-
anni, a thickset Italian, shuffles to and fro between
e tables and the kitchen. He has on a white jacket,
ightly frayed, and a clip-on bow tie. "What do you
commend this evening?" asks Dr. Hesseltine.
Everythingza very good," Giovanni says. A rela-
onship. Over against the wall opposite Mr. Binton
re the remains of a dinner just eaten by my sister
nd me. Two plates probably containing something
hich the Volney menu describes as "Salisbury
teak," and some green stuff, which the Volney menu
alls "Broccoli à la Volney." Also a copy of *Seven-
en,* which my sister has left behind and will pick
p tomorrow evening. My sister and I are back
pstairs. The seventh floor. A four-room suite, so-
alled. A small living room, which contains a couch,
ome chairs, a table, a small desk, where my mother
ays the bills and writes her letters; a bedroom for
y mother and father; a room for my sister; and a
mall room off to the side, which has another desk,
day bed, and is described alternately as my father's
udy, or as his dressing room, or as my room, when
am home from school. My father has been back
om California over a year. He is fifty years old.

157

Has much gray in his hair. Also a cane, and a slight limp (the result of a car accident in Hollywood which soon goes away, although he retains the cane. My sister, now twelve, is lying on her bed. She wears a flowered bathrobe, feet sticking out in white wool socks, her hair in curlers, those little rubber things to get the ringlet effect. She reads a book something about horses; she is keen on horses then will hear no harsh words spoken about horses. My mother is in the bedroom nearby, once her room now (since my father's arrival from England) their room: her own pink pillows upon the bed, a water color of an island scene upon the bedside table, the dressing table filled with jars and bottles. My mother sits at the dressing table: pink slip, stockings, dabbing at her face with bits of things, hair hanging down below her shoulders. A cigarette burns in the ash tray. An Old-Fashioned, sipped at, somewhere near by. My father glides in and out of the small room. My father in shirt and trousers, white silk shirt English trousers ending up somewhere in the small of the back, braces. My mother is holding a dress up against her in front of the mirror. My father glides in. Thick hair combed back, drink in hand. You look-lovely-dear, he says. My mother stares at him. My father glides out. My father discusses horses with my sister. My sister wants to ride in the Grand National. My father describes the cavalry of Genghis Khan. "You should have more light to read by, he says. My sister pulls a face. My father stands in front of the mirror in his-study-dressing-room-my-room, tying his tie. I am in the small slip-covered chair beside the desk, reading a book. The desk is empty, save for a yellow pad, and three pages of a story begun by him six months ago and never finished, a romance between some R.A.F. officer and a nurse, now hidden in one of the small drawers. The tie is silk, gray silk. He ties it with great care. The wide end down and over, like this. Then through the loop. He stops to show me. I watch, half skeptical, half loving. It suddenly all seems very gay somehow, despite the dinginess, the darkened dining room, the tatty gentility. My father puts a small pearl tiepin in his tie. "Come here," he says. "There is a way to do this that doesn't spoil the tie." I come up close. His voice is deep, matter-of-fact, instructive. He moves the tiepin through the silk. I watch his hands, the silk, the tiepin. We are in a canoe together. A fishing trip. My father and I whirl great fly-lines through the air. We cook food together on metal skillets beside the riverbank. He threads the tiepin through, smooths the tie back into place. I feel unbearably happy. My mother appears, fastening an earring onto an ear. She corrects a strand of hair. My father puts on his coat. Good night, good night. My mother tells my sister to read by a better light. The cane, her heels sound in the hallway outside. They wait for James to haul the elevator up.

$\mathcal{E}$ACH SCHOOL VACATION IN NEW YORK there was the ritual of having lunch with Uncle Hugh. Uncle Hugh was not my uncle, or anywhere near it. He was a man called Hugh Payson Courtland (in point of fact, for most of his life Hugh Payson Courtland II, his father having finally, at age ninety-two, removed both himself and his roman numeral), and he was my father's new friend. My father's new American friend. Hugh was a little over six feet. Close to sixty. Silvery-haired. Bright blue eyes. One of those marvelous ruddy Episcopal faces that always looked as if it had just been scoured with a steel brush. Uncle Hugh had himself been to St. Paul's, and Harvard. He had been an aviator in the First World War. He had been some kind of a

lawyer. Now he was some kind of a businessman.
He was a director. He was on "boards." Uncle Hugh
had lots of brothers and cousins, who lived on ances-
tral acres in exotic Englishy-sounding places like Beverly Farms and Bedford Village. Hugh's father apparently had been a long-ago famous New York
senator, and there were countless photographs of the
old gentleman all over Hugh's house, mostly on
horseback. Uncle Hugh was clearly Very Old Family, the near-end-of-the-line in fact of one of those
proud, rich New England families—Hugh himself,
one gathered (from Hugh), represented the more or
less Bohemian, or renegade, aspect of the family;
mostly, it would seem, by having married a French
wife, a pale, decent woman of considerable forbear-
ance. I remember dinners at Hugh's house, a rather
shambly but nicely lived-in brownstone in the East
Seventies, with Marie, his wife, downstairs on the
ground floor, in the kitchen, and Hugh three stories
above in his elegant little library: drinks, cigars, old
books on the shelves, Hugh in his evening clothes
("I think it is good for the morale to dress for
dinner"), Hugh prattling on with his stories—Hugh
was the only man I've ever met whose conversation
consisted entirely of stories. Marie downstairs in her
long dress, it always seemed to be the same dress
too (a long purply thing with a couple of hopeful
strands of silver), Marie down in the engine room
way below, hauling up the ancient Courtland china

161

and the ancient Courtland silver on the dumb-waiter, creak-creak-creak-clank, Hugh and his amusing stories, sounds of creaking rope, Marie hauling up the roast, Marie hauling up the veg, clank-clank, sounds of pulleys, sounds of glasses being rattled. Hugh telling us about the amusing thing that had happened to his Cousin Sandy at a Turkish bagnio in 1922, Marie finally appearing in the doorway to announce dinner, poking pins back into her hair, brushing off her dress, Marie managing a smile, Marie looking as if she had been down at the docks all afternoon unloading sacks of flour and would like just now to go to bed.

I usually felt ill-at-ease alone with Uncle Hugh, mostly because he was always trying to tell me dirty stories, and because I couldn't make much sense of him, although the last I didn't much require. I very much wanted to be friends, though, or whatever it was I was supposed to be with Uncle Hugh, because he was my father's friend; because then he was the only actual friend I was aware of my father having. Our lives, my father's life, had always been peopled for me by these dim far-off shapes of his "old friends," the barely visible outlines of such as Maugham, Noel Coward, Clark Gable, and the like. It didn't bother me that I had almost never seen these men, although naturally it would have pleased me like anything to impress my Wall Street and Oyster Bay schoolmates, sons of Merrill Lynch and Winthrop Stimson, with my acquaintance in the wider world. Mostly it bothered me that my father didn't seem to see them either, or that when he did (one might run into Gary Cooper at the theater, exchange a few words), it seemed like dinghies bumping. Noel Coward would be in town for the opening of a new play. Noel would come by for a drink. Noel admittedly was more of a genuine old friend than the others (my father, I knew, had been one of the key backers for Coward's first play, *The Vortex*), but even so, it seemed that no matter how much gossip and wit and anecdote they nudged across a coffee table at each other every few years, they remained two people clearly in private untouching worlds. I don't know what I expected—Coward and my father on a walking tour of Belgium together, or sharing a Thanksgiving turkey, or drinking a lot and cuffing each other on the shoulder. Uncle Hugh at any rate seemed to have the makings of some kind of visible ordinary friend. For one thing, he came around a lot. He professed to take an interest in our family. He may have been a grade or two off as to what year my sister was in at school, but at least he knew she was at school, and more or less where. And he seemed genuinely to like my father. He and my father "did things together." Other people's fathers, I knew, "did things together" with their friends—playing golf, or cards, or going in a large boat to fish for marlin. My father and Uncle

Hugh, I think, mostly walked back from lunch together. It seemed enough. I remember seeing them
together walking down Fifth Avenue. An October
afternoon. Hugh in a dark suit, gray vest, a bowler
on his head. My father with his cane, no hat. My
father gesticulating with his hand, talking. Hugh
laughing. Comrades. And then, once each school vacation, once each school vacation for at least five
years, Hugh would take me to lunch at the Racquet
Club. I both looked forward to these times, because
having lunch with Hugh Payson Courtland at the
Racquet seemed like such a nice snobby thing to
do, and dreaded them, because I felt that although
Hugh wanted to like me and take-an-interest in me
as part of his role as my father's new friend, in fact
he disapproved of me because I didn't laugh at his
jokes, or worse, laughed in that awful obvious way
of trying not to disappoint the teller. The routine
never varied much. I'd put on my "good suit," try
to find a tie without egg on it, shine the shoes, hop
a bus down to Fifty-third Street, present myself at
the big door always in the hope that the Swiss Guards
who manned the entrance would instinctively assume
me to be a member. Mr. Hugh Payson Courtland
would be waiting in the bar. Much handshaking and
clasping of shoulders. Drinks, a brandy and soda
for Hugh, a beer for me, a brief torrent of jokes and
stories about Hugh's days at St. Paul's. We would
then go to the oyster bar, which I also dreaded,

because I could barely look at oysters or clams in those days without wanting to throw up, but at my first lunch with Hugh I had somehow got myself into the fix of saying, Oh yes, by all means the oyster bar, I love oysters, etc. If I couldn't give him much return on the jokes, at least I wanted to cooperate on the shellfish. And then lunch. A small table by the window. Hugh sitting opposite me. Another avalanche of anecdotes, and then the jokes: I really shouldn't tell you this, Hugh would say with a giggle. And then some damn thing about American aviators and farmers' daughters. Or about President Roosevelt and his secretary. Hugh elaborating on the detail. Me sitting there, gravely, primly (desperately not wanting to be grave or prim), waiting, waiting for the punch line, I must be able to spot the punch line coming, rearrange my face so that my burst-of-helpless-laughter (in reality a sickly grin) will be vaguely plausible. The punch line. The sickly grin. Hugh giggling, giggling, I really used to hate those giggles, that pink face, soft, the eyes all squinched up, the hand reaching across to my arm. "I really shouldn't have told you that." A kind of wink. I once tried to say something of my discomfiture to my father, but it just didn't make any sense to him. Uncle Hugh after all didn't tell dirty jokes to *him*. "Hugh is very naughty," my mother would say sometimes, but I think what she mostly had in mind was Marie and the dumb-waiter. I don't know what it was my father really felt for Hugh. He liked him, I know, because he used to speak of him in a certain way, that simple offhand way that people use when they like someone. I think Hugh must have entertained him, to some degree anyway. Mostly, I'd guess that he found in Hugh, and in Hugh's place in America (Hugh's alleged place in America), some kind of solid object to hold on to, not that he ever seemed to be holding on to it very tightly. I think he probably liked to have it around. And they had good times together.

I remember sitting in class one morning up at St. Paul's, and someone coming in to say that classes were being let out for the next hour for the purpose of listening to two visiting dignitaries who had just come up to address the school. We all filed down into the big study hall, partly pleased at being let out of class, partly wary as to just what in hell was coming next—and there, seated on either side of the great glowing Rector, were Uncle Hugh and my father, grave, serious, terribly serious, in their best Supreme Court manner. And then they spoke, my father first, something about Literature and Life, at least it was supposed to be about that. I remember Aldous Huxley being mentioned, and several stories about Sam Goldwyn—I was too generally dizzy and embarrassed to listen properly, but the faces around me seemed suitably attentive. Some laughs. Applause.

Then Uncle Hugh spoke, something about Paris and Business and Rebuilding Europe, which he seemed to be making up as he went along. Also a success. I went up to see them after it was over, that seeming to be the logical thing to do. They were full of good spirits—had been up in Boston the day before attending some Harvard thing Hugh had been involved in, a big party, a lot of drinking, and somewhere along the line had decided to come up to the school and lecture at it. We had lunch at the small inn nearby, my father and Hugh congratulating each other on the fine reception accorded their talks, the attentive quality of the students, the general splendidness of young-people-today, and so forth, both of them extremely pleased with themselves. It was very nice. We all had brandy after lunch, which gave me a warm buzz between the ears, and then they went back to New York. It was the first time, now that I think of it, that my father had ever been to the school.

My father had one other friend around that time, whom I've almost forgotten because after my father died he moved right out of our lives. His name was Nadal, André Nadal. He was Iranian, I think. Some generations back anyway. A dark tall man, with a bushy mustache. Thick brown curling hair. A kind face. He was an immigration inspector and he lived somewhere in Queens. I think my father had met him when he'd first arrived from England—I don't know much about the connection beyond that, except that for a long while in New York the only two people, *friends,* I could have imagined "dropping by" for Thanksgiving dinner (if one had been having Thanksgiving dinner) would have been André and Uncle Hugh. André I think of as a truly gentle man, with one of those lovely, warm, seemingly untroubled laughs. He would sometimes come by for lunch when my father kept that table at the St. Regis, taking his place quietly along with the others, the flashy talkers, the great English-suited figures, the Rockefeller Center boulevardiers—André seated there listening, saying a few words, the rumpled brown suit, the long hair, André laughing. And then when the others would leave, André would stay on with my father, and sort of gently chide him for his frivolities. Not chide him very much. I think of André as being an intelligent, sensitive man, and the only man I can myself recall who used to talk seriously to my father about "life," and things like that. André was very proud of his job; of "government"; of being in the civil service. I remember once our families all had dinner on a summer evening. André took us out to the Tavern-on-the-Green—André; his wife, a nice large lady who seemed even friendlier than André; their daughter, a girl of about ten; and the four of us. I think we may have had one or two other dinners together, but I just happen to remember that one. I don't really remember very much about it. My father talked about his brother Taki, and his family in England. André talked about Government, and the "role of Congress." Everyone seemed very happy. Some seven or eight years later, at the funeral service for my father, I remember seeing André coming into the chapel, standing alone at the back. I went over towards him—it had been a long while since I had seen him, since any of us had gotten together. He was just standing in the back, a bit the way he used to sit there in the St. Regis, the only man there as far as I could see who seemed to be shedding the kind of tears that actually make you wet.

$\mathcal{B}$LUE WATER. THE MEDITERRANEAN. The faint blue you could glimpse down through the trees at Cannes. The blue-green water off the rocks at Antibes. My father's dark hair below me off the rocks at Eden Roc. Black rocks. Umbrellas open beneath the sun. The water is very clear. My father moves slowly, ten feet below, a far distance, treading water, a sort of breast stroke. A blue bathing suit. He, like most of the men, has recently given up the top to his bathing suit. My mother is nearby somewhere, beneath one of the umbrellas. There is nobody else in the water. "Come on in, jump," my father says. Also the beach at Cannes: in front of the hotels. A narrow strip of sand. I think of the sand as being gray. The great garish faces of the hotels lined up behind it. The Carlton. Majestic. The Miramar. The beach strewn with children and with nannies. White starched uniforms. Standing upright on the sand. There were lifeguards and swimming instructors. One of them, I remember, a German, blond and tanned. He had a long bamboo pole, like a fishing pole, with a tire of sorts, maybe an inner tube, attached to the end of it. He stood at the end of the dock. One was told to climb inside the inner tube, hold on. And then flung off the dock. He was very hearty and believed in physical fitness, and I never asked what else. There were sailboats in the harbor. Sometimes a submarine. The English battle cruiser *Hood* appeared one day, peacetime maneuvers, moored five miles off. My father was invited out to tea one afternoon, took me along. I had an interest in ships. There was a mess table laid out on one of the forward decks. White tablecloth. Tea. Cakes. The great gray guns overhead. The little sailboats back against the harbor. There were shellfish along the beach. Sponge and coral in the sea. We took a sailboat down the coast to Italy one summer. My mother's cousin was along. He wore a bright blue blazer. A small harbor somewhere. Lemon houses. We stayed mostly on the boat. The captain fished. He chopped up little bits of squid for bait, put them on hooks. My father water-skied. Blue water. Outside the harbor, the waves chopped against the sides of the boat. We sailed all night one night.

171

And then there was one summer we went to the mountains. It was a place in Austria, in the Tyrol, called Semmering. I don't know why we went there now, I suppose my parents wanted a change. We took the train out of Cannes one evening. I remember all of us on the platform: my parents, my small sister, the nanny (Nanny Nye)—and then suddenly Monsieur Puigue, the chef, our chef, and the whole staff, came hurtling onto the platform in an old pick-up truck, all of them (not that there were that many) looking a bit dazed, as if they had just been tumbled out of bed, Monsieur Puigue in charge of the show, Monsieur Puigue still in his white apron, little thin mustache, presenting something to my mother in a box, a cake, much waving of arms, expressions of gratitude, affection, and then we were off. We stopped for hours at the Italian border. Some nuns got on at Genoa. My sister threw up a lot. In Venice, my father took us all to lunch at the Grand Hotel, which must have been a treat for him. Nanny Nye bought postcards. They put the electric engine on somewhere inside the Austrian border, an immense fat brutish thing, and for what seemed like several days we wound up into the mountains, steep faces of red rock, pine trees, tunnels. Semmering was a kind of spa. We stayed in the big hotel, which was full of Austrians, Germans, and English businessmen. There didn't seem much to do. My sister and I went for walks in the hillside meadows, and into the forests that grew down the mountains. Once, I remember, we walked quite far, through very dark glades, wildflowers, mushrooms, occasional bright patches of sunlight that seemed even more disturbing than the darkness. There were some big buildings. We went inside one of them. A great dark room. Huge. A gymnasium. All sorts of strange equipment. Machines made up to look like animals. Large leather contraptions that seemed to run on electricity. And suddenly through one of the far doors a double line of boys and girls marching in step. Fourteen, fifteen years old. All tanned, beautiful. White shirts, trousers, white tunics. They formed a square. An older boy stood in front of them. They did calisthenics and then sang. I don't remember what they sang.

In the course of that summer, my sister and I became quite close. For one thing, Nanny Nye was old, and fell asleep much of the afternoons. We were also bored with Semmering and made plans to run away. One day after lunch, I swiped some rolls from the dining room, a bar of chocolate from my parents' room—my sister and I went down the hill-side, down the meadows, rocks, small pine trees, slithering, all those dark glades. I remember pulling her after me, she was very small and blond, held on to my hand. She was excited by all the chocolate. We left the road, the path, went down through the trees. The hill became very steep; it was a mountain

173

really. We fell a lot. Brambles. I had never been so far away before. And then there was a larger road. I think I had some idea it would lead to Vienna, which was about a hundred miles away. A big touring car came by, stopped. Wide running boards, windshield. A man got out. A tall German chauffeur. He opened the back door of the car, motioned to us to get in. We got in. Going back in that car, it didn't seem as if we had been far away at all. Soon the driveway. The hotel. We weren't allowed to go on walks alone for the rest of the week, which meant we had to play in the dreadful hotel playground on the swings and seesaws. Sometimes in the late afternoon then, my sister and I would sit on the balcony outside the Gramophone Room and watch the train from Vienna coming around the side of the mountain opposite us. There was a certain time and place that it always appeared, a glint of sunlight on the great engine. The mountains really were beautiful, although too grand. I tried collecting rocks, then lizards. Towards the end of summer there was a tennis tournament at the hotel, which was won by a businessman from Wales. His name was Llewellyn, which I remember because he had a son called David. David Llewellyn. We were never close friends, but after dinner we would sometimes sit outside on the lawn and talk. About battleships mostly, and airplanes. He said he had seen tanks in Germany. I said I had seen tanks in France. There was a big dance in the hotel one night. The women all in evening dresses. Japanese lanterns. An orchestra from Vienna played fox-trots and waltzes.

$\mathcal{M}$Y SISTER AT SEVENTEEN. MY SISTER at seventeen is actually a nice-looking girl: blond hair (which after all those years in curlers she now wears straight and in a pageboy;) blue eyes; what is described as a "good figure," which means nice breasts, which I feel I am not supposed to notice but dart astonished and unsettling looks at anyway; about my mother's height, which in fact is on the short side if you discount the pile of hair atop the head, but without my mother's coiffure or Lady Windermere bearing, and without confidence, which blows everything. "I don't feel very attractive," she confesses to me at times, although I am not much of a person to confess this sort of thing to then, my own self-confidence being such that were I able to change my

own un-American face into Gary Cooper's left el-
bow I would gladly do so. I mumble something off
into her direction, continue to take batting swings
in front of my mirror, have vivid dreams of Ava
Gardner, impotence, fertility, sterility, think stead-
fastly about myself. "Oh, definitely attractive," my
mother tells her helpfully, "although not beautiful."
My sister sits in her room a lot (which she has been
allowed to paint the color of her choice, pale blue),
plays Ella Fitzgerald records on the record player,
takes baths throughout the day. *My Funnee Val-en-
tine* . . . Bathwater running. My sister lies on her
bed in a white quilted robe, her feet in furry slippers,
says she would rather know the straight truth about
her looks than be led on by vain dreams and delu-
sions. My sister also worries about her eyes, which
are on the weak side, and cause her to wear reading
glasses. She also worries about her nose, which she
suddenly considers too large. My father agrees, in
what one imagines he regards as a friendly fashion.
Father taking an interest. My sister's nose is in fact
a fine nose, a fine Armenian nose, which in the wom-
en runs admittedly a bit to width, and most closely
resembles that of my father's sister, Ahavni, that of
his sister-in-law, Anais, and indeed to some degree
his own. "You should have it bobbed," he says to
her one evening. My sister smiles bravely. Father taking an interest. There is talk of the silent-film star
Carmel Meyers, and of her nose-changing operation

—of some *mot* my father had delivered at the time (about cutting off one's nose to spite one's race), which had caused him to be banished from several homes in Hollywood. Laughter. There is talk of Ahavni. Of Ahavni's nose. "It's only a small operation . . ." my mother is saying. "They have excellent doctors," my father says. "All they do is remove a small bone. Somewhere in here." He pats his nose. My sister sits there opposite me, between them, tears streaming down her face. She runs from the room. "I'll never do it, I'll never do it," she sobs later, face down on the bed. On the table beside the bed is a clock-radio I had given her for Christmas, a glass of beer, a copy of *Gone with the Wind,* which she is re-reading for the eighth or ninth time. She gets to her feet, goes over to the mirror, peers at her face, which is now puffy from crying. "I'll never do it," she says. "It's not so bad." The subject is dropped. "You'd think we were trying to force her into an operation," my father said some time afterwards, when noses were again fleetingly mentioned.

$\mathcal{B}$Y THE END OF MY LAST YEAR AT ST.
Paul's, all the things I most wanted to be I wasn't.
I wanted to be a great school athlete and win the
revered Gordon medal (presented the day before
graduation at a special ceremony around the flag-
pole by old Mr. Gordon himself). I would have
settled for being what was known as "extremely popular" (a quality much admired in those days, as I
guess "personality" was in girls), a leader of the
school, an important figure on the student council
—one of the four Sixth Form toffs who sat in special
ornamented seats in chapel, just in front of the special ornamented seats of the Rector and Vice-Rector.
None of these signal honors seemed in the cards, or
anywhere near it, although life there on the whole

179

didn't seem too bad, mostly because the school was then (and I imagine now) so full of the kind of young men I admired very much: young men who could play hockey very well, or squash, or who could kick 25-yard field goals at crucial moments, and who owned cars on the side, and sometimes sailboats, and had summer houses as well as ordinary houses. There was a time, quite a long time in fact, when I think I envied nearly anyone who had a house—well, not really any house. If pressed closely on the subject, I think it would turn out that what I chiefly envied were people who had houses in places like Greenwich and Old Westbury. Marvelous desirable Greenwich! O great wondrous mowed lawns! And little boats at Indian Harbor! Club memberships! Yacht Club parties! The heady presence of older girls ("women") who went to Smith, and older men ("men") who went to Yale and Princeton. And all those beautiful red-faced, flush-nosed Wall Street Dads (no damn Daddy nonsense there), with their billowy sports coats, and fuchsia slacks, and brand-new Chryslers, and elaborate bars with electric ice-smashers, and hearty laughs, and jokes, and deep grave interest in the Yale football team—and all those blond, well blondish, Mums, or Moms, or Mothers, with their sleek county look, their cashmeres, stationwagons, teensie-weensie drinkies in the evening, *their* equally deep grave interest in the Yale football team! I stayed close to all these people, or tried to stay close. Roomed with the more lustrous athletes. On vacations, tried to be adopted by their parents in Connecticut or Long Island. About all I really thought I had going for me then was that I was a "good student," but even that I secretly believed to be a sham. Not so much the factual, the achievement part. I knew I was a good student because I had the grades to prove it. St. Paul's, in those days at any rate, was a great believer in the authority and importance of grades. Once a month the "ranking list" of each form was tacked on to the main bulletin board, the name of every boy in the school listed on immense sheets of graph paper and, beside his name, the grade he had received in each subject figured out to the nearest decimal point, such as 88.7 (being naturally a better grade than 88.6). On the whole I was very good at this sort of thing— getting good grades. In truth I had no idea, or very little idea, of whether I was intelligent or not. For the most part, I believed I wasn't—but I knew how to study very hard. I knew, for example, that if I painstakingly underlined and then wrote out the correct meaning of every word in my Latin homework I didn't know, and then looked at them over and over again, and over again, I would get them right. And then the results of all this pleased my father very much. He liked for me to do well at school, to get good grades. In fact, he counted on me to do well. Each vacation time the reports would be mailed home. "History: 84.5. He continues to show an interest in the subject and has a strong grasp of the information. But his essays lately have shown a tendency to be unsure and general . . ." I see the history is down a bit, my father would say. Yes, I guess so, I'd say. Then: It's all that stuff after Napoleon. It doesn't seem very interesting. Not interesting! he'd say. That's a curious explanation. After Napoleon? The Second Empire? I thought history was one of your best subjects, etc. And so forth. He took an interest. And I did too most of the time. But then in the spring of my last term there I began to slack off. Or rather, I just stopped taking all those pains. No special reason; maybe just being the last term, spring, sunshine, end-of-school. And then, scant weeks before examinations, I realized that my beautiful grades had dropped considerably in the past month's rankings, and that from the way things were going I wasn't going to emerge with honors at graduation even as a student, which admittedly seemed a poor third to the Gordon medal, or being on the council, but which I knew would be a good deal better than nothing.

There were a number of prizes to be awarded each graduation, and while most of them were for the high hurdles or hockey or something of the sort, a few were for "scholarship," and of these one of the better was called the Baxter Prize for History, which in some corner of my mind I had always reserved for myself. And so I decided to really study for it, because in actual fact I had had a pretty good chance of winning it, only now my monthly grades were down so that I would have to do extraordinarily well on the exam (and my rivals would have to do very much less well) for me to pull it off.

All the exams were scheduled for the final week of school, with history on the last day; and so, while paying some small attention to the other subjects, I allotted myself, each day, every day, a certain amount of time for reading over the history book. It was the standard Morison & Commager American history text: a big blue thing. Two volumes. The exam would be on the second volume. Most everyone studied in their rooms or in the library, but I would go over to the schoolhouse right after dinner, the big red-brick building with most of the classrooms, which was supposed to be unoccupied at night, and hole up in a back room—hard wooden chairs, one of those circular tables, blackboards, maps, charts of chemical elements, travel posters of the Loire. I re-read every word in Morison & Commager. And then I re-read it again. I tried to imagine what the questions might be, and then I'd seek out the relevant chapters, and just gaze at each page, page after page, late at night, sometimes no longer knowing what I was reading, what I was doing, until two or three in the morning when my eyes were so blurred, and I was so tired, that I'd pack up and go back to my room half a mile away, where my hockey-playing roommates were fast asleep. I remember taking the exam that final day, the day before the two-day graduation ceremonies began, and when my parents were due up. It didn't seem too difficult an exam, and I thought I'd done well; at least I'd written it very rapidly, which was usually a good sign, and with a sense of what I was doing. Anyway it was over. I suddenly wanted terribly much to get the prize, and I figured I had a fair chance. My mother and father were due in around noon. There was to be a track meet and crew races in the afternoon. Sometime while all that was going on, Mr. Harding was going to post the history results. I was pleased about but rather wary of my parents' arrival. Originally I hadn't wanted them to come up. Not so much because of the usual filial embarrassment, although I certainly felt some of that. Mostly because their actual physical presence reminded me that I couldn't realistically hope to be adopted into one of those beautiful county families in Greenwich or Long Island—I already had parents of my own; and in fact there they were, walking down the brick walk beside the schoolhouse, two figures clearly different from all the others who had just now come into view—no billowy sports coat on him, no B. H. Wragge on her, no Old St. Paul's blazer, no straw hats, no jolly laugh, no jolly group: a short dark man with a mustache, an excessively tailored suit, a cane (he'd

brought a cane, for God's sake!), and a woman with
an exotic hairdo, also a tailored suit, and a kind of
presence that seemed both to advertise and disregard
her total ignorance of football at Yale, or anywhere
else. We went through the usual peculiar ceremonies
of greeting-in-public. "What do you want to do?"
I'd say. Shifting from one foot to the other. Hands
thrust into pockets, thrust out of pockets. "But it's
your school," they'd say. "You show us." Benign.
Cooperative. The elders of the tribe remind the young
brave that it's *his* Initiation Rite, after all. "Surely
you don't want to see the crew race!" I'd say wildly.
My mother would beam as if I had just proposed a
moonlight visit to the Taj Mahal. "Crew race? But of
course we want to see the crew race. We certainly
don't want to miss that. Your uncle was once on the
crew at Balliol . . ." and so forth. And off we would
go, me staring at the ground, nodding distractedly at
friends ("That nice boy seemed to be trying to speak
to you . . ."), some yellow rented schoolbus to take
us all out to the pond, hearty alumni in old crew
blazers, my friends, their parents, younger brothers
—and there we all were on the banks of Long Pond,
my mother and father standing on a little hillock of
grass, my father leaning casually on his cane. "Is
there any particular boat we should cheer for?"
Cheer for? My sense of lunacy and gloom would
deepen. It seemed quite bad enough that they should
suddenly be there. Visible. But audible too! Cheer-

ing! The boat races proceeded. Two little eight-oared shells nudging down the middle of the dark-blue pond. A handful of motorboats trailing behind. It was too far away to see much of anything. Loud cheering from the bank. "Come on, Shattuck! Come on, Halcyon!" (The names of the two rowing clubs.) My father was talking with Mr. Enfield, the Latin master. The importance of a Classical Education, and so forth. My mother seemed to be staring into the middle distance with a sort of contented bafflement. I looked out at the boats, privately thought they were both marvelous, and worried desperately about the history exam. Finally, the races were over, we went back to the school. I ducked my parents—they were going to some tea at the Rector's house, I didn't even bother to worry whether or not they would embarrass me there—and ran over to the schoolhouse, where the grades would be posted.

On the bulletin board there was a brand-new list. My form. History. I looked at it, found my name, felt a wild feeling of apprehension and excitement, read across the graph-paper line towards the grades. Zero. 0. I couldn't believe it. Zero. Nobody got zero. I read quickly down the column of numbers. Everyone else had done pretty much as expected. Holmes, my chief rival, had an 89. I had zero. I felt quite sick, saw some people coming, ran out the door. I wandered around the back of the schoolhouse for a bit, not knowing what to do, hoping dimly that if I wandered around enough the zero would somehow change itself, which it didn't. Then I went over to see Mr. Harding. He had a small suite of rooms in one of the Fifth Form houses. I wasn't sure whether I wanted him to be in or not. I knocked at the heavy brown door. Silence. I was about to go away, then knocked again. The door opened. Harding appeared. Gray baggy trousers. Dark vest. Gold watch chain in the vest. He must have been around fifty then, although he seemed older. Thin gray hair. Straight nose. Eyes that were very clear, and sometimes kind. "I don't understand about the exam . . ." I began. I must have been very close to tears. "What don't you understand?" said Harding. I was sitting in a small chair beside his desk. He seemed very cold, remote. "The zero," I said. "The grade." Harding reached over for a stack of blue books, riffled through them, produced what seemed to be mine. A large, unmistakable zero in red crayon had been inscribed on the cover. "I think the grade should be perfectly clear," Harding said. Then: "I am not a fool, you know." I looked at him dumbly. Then: "The answer to the essay question that you have written here is an exact word-for-word transcription of pages 94 through 97 in *The History of the American Republic.*" He more or less flung the exam book at me. I opened it, looked through it with thick fingers, not really seeing anything, even my own handwriting seemed strange to me—felt sick, felt very scared,

187

began to cry, then eventually tried to explain. All I could say really was that I hadn't cheated. Sir, sir, I hadn't cheated. I had just studied very hard. I had (it seemed) studied so hard, or relentlessly, or stupidly, that I'd in fact memorized the bloody textbook. We went on like that for a while. Then Harding stood up and went over to a shelf. He produced a fresh exam book and put it in front of me. "All right," he said. "You will sit here and write me the same answer to the essay question that you so kindly gave me yesterday. I will now repeat the question." He leaned against the side of the small leaded window, closed his eyes, unrolled the question, which I remember had to do with Woodrow Wilson, the League of Nations, and the period just after the First War. "You have thirty minutes," he said, and left the room. For whole moments, minutes, endless minutes, I just stared dumbly at the exam book in front of me. I opened it. Stared at the blank page. The inside of my head seemed absolutely inert. Woodrow Wilson. The League of Nations. I was supposed to remember and write out a 700-word or so stretch of text that I hadn't even known I'd memorized some days ago. Eventually I began to write. I began somewhere, and just wrote. Some of the phrases seemed familiar, plausible. Some of it was blind. I wrote on and on, and finished. I called out to Mr. Harding that I was done. He was in the other room.

"All right," I heard him say, but he seemed not to be coming nearer, and so I left.

I went back to try to find my parents at the Rectory. Everybody I passed or met, I felt sure, was looking at me. Everybody *knew*. My parents must surely know. I saw them talking with Mr. Francis, who was the Vice-Rector. They all looked very grave. I felt absolutely sick. "Mr. Francis has been explaining to us about the summer teaching program," my father said, in his new-found parent-teacher voice. I stayed with them, silent, fearful. Later, at dinner, the three of us in the little tearoomy inn, a din of parents, old graduates, boys around us, I longed to tell them of my misfortune, my disgrace, but couldn't bear to. "Is something wrong?" my father asked at some point. "No," I said. "He's probably tired," my mother said. Before going back to my house, my father and I took a short walk down beside the Lower School pond. It was one of the places I'd liked most at St. Paul's. Not a big pond at all, quite gardened and tended-to on the near side, where we were walking; but on the far side, full of coves and inlets, tall wild clumps of rushes, reeds, small swampy places, hidden places. In my Fifth Form year, George Brock and I had kept a small beat-up rowboat hidden there, an old thing that barely floated but that we'd patched up somehow, and spent what had seemed like most of the spring aboard it, fishing late at night, smoking, discussing the true meanings of life, hockey, sex. My father seemed intent on talking to me about a summer job. "I think it's time you began to get into something," he said. And: "Now that you're older . . ." he said. I paced beside him, trying to be manly, glancing out mournfully at the darkened pond. Ah, the simple past! George and I had bought a fishing rod in Concord one afternoon, quite an elaborate, expensive fly-fishing thing, and used to try to instruct each other in the evening, standing knee-deep in mud and swamp, the pond eventually lit only by stars and half a moon, the fly-line whistling, singing above one's head, landing inevitably in trees and bushes, landing in bulrushes, now and then, invisibly, unnoticed, upon the water. "Fantastic, fantastic," George would say. "Don't make a sound for Christ's sakes!" (I never figured out what role silence was supposed to play at those moments.) Now I walked beside this pond, beside my father, feeling him not at all, listening in a way quite placidly to his admonitions about summer work, but with only this one thought in my mind, of Harding's zero. I knew I didn't want to tell my father about it. It wasn't that I was uncertain whether he would understand or not; I didn't even take it that far. I just didn't want to tell him. We walked along. I said I agreed, a summer job would be a good thing. I said I'd thought of trying to get a job as crew aboard Dave Whitney's sloop. "That's not the kind of summer job I had in mind," he said. We talked a bit about the new apartment in New York, about my sister, about my cousin Sarkis who had been visiting, and then said good night in front of the inn. Good night, good night, a light male-to-male brush of the cheek. I went back to my room. My roommates were all up, all very cheery. I went into the bedroom, undressed, got into bed, turned towards the wall, tried all night to sleep.

The next day, graduation in the afternoon—well, the story has a happy ending, this one anyway, although when I look back on it, it all seems foolish, no one comes out of it in any strong light, except possibly for old Harding. He'd decided to believe me at any rate—the second exam I'd written had turned out to be more or less exactly like the first. This still left him, and me, with the problem of my having answered a history exam more or less by rote. He gave me a 90, which is what I'd usually had (except for the past two months), and this got me the Baxter Prize. I remember that evening sitting between my mother and father in the study hall, the cavernous Middle School study hall where the prizes were awarded. Row upon row of wooden chairs. Everybody's beautiful parents on either side of me. Masters in their black robes. Some girls. The whole world seemed to have returned to life. My great good friend, Harry Thompson, the wondrous hockey player, sat two rows behind me, between his mother and stepfather, and stepmother and father.

His father, Harry Thompson II, had also been a
wondrous hockey player, although I gathered that
he had been "too light for the Varsity" at Yale. We
waved, exchanged cheery greetings between the
awards. Charlie Prescott had already received the
Gordon medal, which was no surprise to anyone.
Dick Vandiver, head of the student council (re-
portedly so mature that he had to shave twice a
day) received the Merrick Prize. Some other prizes.
The Charles Henderson Hubbard Prize "for that boy
who, in his qualities of sportsmanship, leadership,
and school spirit, most resembles the late Charles
Henderson Hubbard," and so forth. The Baxter
Prize for History. Me. The Rector resplendent as
the Pope of Rome upon the platform, two books
thrust into my hand. My parents were very pleased.
"Interesting books, too," my mother said. Afterwards, Harry Thompson, especially wondrous in his
blazer, hair wetted down, huge long arms, inartic-
ulate, introduced me to his parents, then in a wild
fit of politesse introduced all his parents and semi-
parents to mine. "And this is my mother, and this
is Fred White . . . and this is my dad . . . and this
is Jane . . ." Jane, the stepmother, an elegant
suburban Theda Bara whom I greatly admired for
her charm and sophistication, discussed packing and
the size of suitcases with my mother. Harry Thompson II clasped my father around the shoulders and

looked happy. It was all very gay. The next morning, the cars began to drive up to the dormitories. Some with chauffeurs, mostly not. Harry's father had a big green convertible. A trunk and hockey sticks and records and baseball gloves were loaded in. My mother and father and I went back by train, a nice trip really, we stopped at Boston, had lunch at the Ritz. My father talked about the importance of having a "really good education," and about the Rector, who was always trying to tell him of his deep admiration for the English people. We laughed a lot, the three of us. I remember the thick blue goblets they used as water glasses, and still think of them with pleasure.

It was several more years, well into college, before I stopped trying to memorize things, and then it wasn't by any decision, I just stopped. I guess I dimly began to be aware that my mind had a life, an existence of its own. A couple of years ago, though, one of my daughters, who was studying something in school about the War of 1812, asked me a question about the shipping trade between England and the Caribbean colonies, and I found myself answering with a column of statistics, average annual tonnage, molasses, rum, Jamaica, London, Boston, that I remember having memorized in the Fourth Form at St. Paul's, when we studied those things too. But maybe the statistics were wrong, at least I rather hope so; I stopped in mid-sentence anyway, told her I didn't know, that she should look it up. One more small thing: I wrote a story about that incident once, the incident with Harding, the prize, graduation. It was the first story I ever sold, right after college. I had it pretty much the way it all had happened, only in my story (it wasn't much of a story) the boy did manage to tell his father. They walked down along beside the pond, and then he told his father, who was angry at first, for a "brief instant." And then clasped the boy to him. The mother had blond hair, green eyes, and was called Nancy.

*M*Y MOTHER WAS NEVER MUCH FOR
reminiscing about herself. By which I mean that
Thanksgiving, for example, was never one of those
opportunities for everyone to sit around the table
singing and drinking and crying and eating, with the
old folk periodically lurching off into remembrances
of bygone festivities and familial happenings. Now
that I think of it, Thanksgiving in our house wasn't
much of an opportunity even for eating, my mother
having no use for turkey, and my father professing
not to understand whether pumpkin pie was a des-
sert or a vegetable, and neither of them really caring
very much for the holiday in the first place, which
I suspect they observed more in the spirit of natu-
ralized citizens paying their first taxes than out of any
great desire to connect themselves more deeply into

American mythology. In any case, I hardly ever remember my mother sitting down with us and launching into one of those when-I-was-a-girl or when-I-was-a-boy things that most people, I find, myself very much included, will do at the drop of a child's question. It wasn't that my mother seemed anxious to erase her past, her childhood, to pretend it hadn't existed. To the contrary, in fact. At times, and especially as my sister and I grew older, she seemed quite desperate to convey to us something, if not of her own identity (whatever that may have been), at any rate of the texture of her past life, her own life; as if suspecting that my sister and I, in our all-too-evident attempts to Americanize ourselves, our all-too-evident acquiring of baseball mitts and bobby-sox, were also at the same time trying to erase *her*. She almost never spoke discursively about herself, and usually refused to answer personal questions if pressed—at times with a kind of genuine embarrassment (who would really want to know about *that?*), at times with an equally genuine pride and sense of privacy, let's keep the children out of that room anyway. But every so often she'd throw out clues. One evening I remember my sister muttering random complaints about the amount of homework she had to do, and my mother, more or less in the act of passing through the room, saying "You oughtn't to complain so much about school, I never went to school"—which wasn't exactly fair to the

subject of homework, since my mother had certainly
had a succession of governesses for most of her life,
and had indeed gone to school briefly a couple of
times (there had been some sort of "finishing school"
in Switzerland when she was seventeen); but it
was nonetheless true to her own feelings about it,
and in any case was the first time that either my
sister or I had been let in to that considerable seg-
ment of her life. And then both of us later trying
to pursue the subject. Gosh, tell us about all those
times you never went to school—and my mother
resolutely dismissing the whole business. "Oh, *that!*"
she'd say. In this diffident, prideful, hit-and-run way,
my mother served up to us selected portions of her
past existence, bits and pieces that she doubtless
cared about, and which it must have pained her that
we couldn't have somehow guessed at. Couldn't have
either ignored or known about intuitively. I can't
imagine, for example, *her* mother ever having sat
down with her and having a serious talk about who
she was, and where she'd been to, and the fact that
my mother now could do it, even to this small degree,
with her own children, has come to seem to me
rather gallant and adventurous. I knew, for instance,
that my mother had once been good at sports, at a
time when very few women were, when it was
only then being discovered that "sportswoman" was
an enhancing adjective, could be a sexy concept—
not entirely limited to photographs of Babe Didrik-

son throwing the javelin at the Olympics. She and I played tennis a lot in the summers, until I was about sixteen anyway. She was quite okay too, a lot of very solid low flat baseline stuff, a lot of running too, a fair backhand, not a bad serve. (Cautions and bad temper at the net.) Now and then, apropos of nothing much, she'd toss out clues about this part of her life—"the summer your uncle and I played in the doubles tournament at Nice." Or: swimming-between-the-islands. Or: "the winter Lillia got sick and we had to ski out twenty miles to the doctor . . ." Then, having placed the object, as it were, upon the table—not as an ability at something, but as an indication of a certain point of view, a feel for life— the object, the clue, would be taken off, brushed to the floor. I remember one summer afternoon at the Homestead, in Hot Springs—we'd just been playing tennis, she and I, three sets of singles on a hot afternoon, and were sitting under one of the elegant umbrellas. The tennis pro had come by, one of those leathery, wiseguy club-athletes. Forty-eight-year-old virility. Misplaced charm. Later she murmured something about Suzanne Lenglen, the great French player in the twenties, *her* father who used to be the pro at the Carlton, and, as if forgetting herself, slipped into an account of some doubles game they'd all played one afternoon in Cannes—and then stopped. It wasn't a name-dropping story, a self-advertising story. Anyway she stopped, and then afterwards when I asked her, quite diplomatically I thought (I was really interested), about Mlle Lenglen and tennis and about the tournament in Nice and so forth, she looked at me as if I'd made the whole thing up, and then said, "I don't know, I don't remember."

The one area in my mother's life that I couldn't figure out at all, and used to think about a certain amount as I got older, sixteen, seventeen, was men. I couldn't for the life of me imagine what sort of life with men my mother had had before she was married, what sort of sexual life, what sort of any life. I know she would have been outraged to think that I was thinking about such matters, as indeed she would be outraged now, but the fact is I was, and that was that. I can't say I thought about it very much—considering the amount of time I devoted to thinking about my own sexual life, or lack of it, I didn't have very much time left over for thinking about anyone else's. But one of the things that mystified me was this apparent contrast between my mother's evident sexuality, which seemed so strong and earthy, and the quite girlish ways with which she seemed to clothe *her* sense of her presence in the world of men. To begin with, there hadn't really been men—there had been "beaux." The names of certain men would crop up in conversations. Somebody marrying somebody. Somebody dying, arriving. Somebody glimpsed somewhere. Oh yes, Freddie. He was an old beau. Hugo was once a beau. Henri was a beau. Each time my mother said the word, each time she connected it to one of these invisible men, I had this picture of some Oxford undergraduate, pink blazer, straw boater, strawberry smile, my mother in a kind of 1919 garden-party frock, the two of them strolling-beside-the-Isis, sound of mandolins, pretty, pretty . . . It didn't make any sense to me. It seemed to me that my mother probably wasn't *pretty* in those ways. I didn't know, of course. I didn't know what any of it had been like. My father sometimes referred to women whom he had been "in love with" before he and my mother were married—Nancy Cunard, Marilyn Miller, Louise Carnarvon—and it never occurred to me that any relationship he had had with, say, Marilyn Miller, and which he was agreeable to describing as "love," could have consisted in its entirety of strolling along riverbanks together, or sending her boxes of candy. Besides, there were always the books. You could find out a lot from books. As a kid I can remember reading in some book of literary prattle by Beverly Nichols or somebody about a Christmas party given by my parents in Cannes, and thus finding out that my father was indeed Santa Claus. Or vice versa. A few years later, at school, I can remember reading in a biography of D. H. Lawrence about an "affair" my father had had with Lady So-and-so. Hey, what's an affair? I asked brightly. "It's when two self-indulgent people have an infatuation with one another," said Mr. Waddington, the English master, "and it usually ends badly." So much for affairs. My parents, at any rate, seemed always very much of the flesh, which was less troubling for what I could imagine than for what I couldn't, or could only imagine with difficulty. My mother and her "beaux." Freddie Chatham. In *bed* with Freddie Chatham! The beast with two backs with Freddie Chatham? Old Freddie Chatham. It wasn't just a question of age. "Freddie's in town for a few days," my mother would say. "Such a sweet little man. He's coming for drinks." Could it be possible that my mother and sweet little Freddie Chatham had once made love, had touched, had flown to the moon together in some flat off Chester Square, in a hayfield, in Hampstead Heath, on the back seat of a bicycle, anywhere —instead of just strolling forever arm-in-arm along the banks of the Isis? "Atalanta, so nice to see you," Freddie would say on arrival. "What marvelous *parquet.*" Freddie at sixty-three. That drawl. The beautiful smooth cheeks. The beautiful lemon-colored cuffs, which seemed to support the wrist, which barely seemed to support the drink. None of it seemed possible. And so, if not Freddie, who?

ONE SPRING VACATION, down from Harvard, I remember two things happening. To begin with, my sister, in perhaps her strongest bid yet at Americanizing herself, had lately expressed a wish to marry a boy called Leroy Taylor. He really was a boy, about nineteen, and his name really was Leroy, which made it doubly, no triply, difficult. Each time my father would speak his name, which he did with a mixture of consummate politeness and disbelief, my sister would break into tears. He was a nice guy, too, studying "business administration" at Babson, rather tall, and skinny, and hopelessly free from guile (also from some of the harder intelligences). Leroy would come down from Boston on vacations and take my sister to basketball games. The N.C.A.A. championships. After the game, they would come home and play Tony Bennett records, and sometimes sit around the library and engage in conversation with my parents. "Mr. Arlen, did you play basketball in high school?" I remember Leroy asking one evening, and my father replying, in really (for him) a reasonably natural and friendly manner, No, he never had, and Leroy saying something about how he guessed height was an important factor, and standing up to show his comparatively extreme height, and my father looking at him in a strange way and saying, "That's very interesting, Leroy," and my sister saying, "Stop it, both of you," and beginning to cry. Then one weekend she went up to visit Leroy's parents in Providence. Then another weekend. The third weekend she announced she wanted to get married—I was home on vacation and I can remember listening in my room one evening (it was all so loud you didn't have to go down and sit on the stairs) to my mother and sister doing what is known as "thrashing it out," which meant in actual fact that my eighteen-year-old sister was issued a paper sword and a clockwork horse, and my mother sat twelve miles offshore and lobbed heavy shells at her for a couple of hours. At one point, though, in the proceedings, I remember my mother saying, "Have you gone to bed with him?" and my sister saying, all sobs and defenses, no, no, she hadn't. "You *haven't* gone to bed with him?" My mother suddenly surprised, angry. My sister still saying no. You little fool, my mother saying, and then much more—about all the "little girls" and "little boys" who rush into marriage just so they can sleep with each other. It sounds pretty sensible as I write it down here; in fact the logic of it is indeed sensible, as little girls and little boys are maybe finally beginning to find out. But then, that evening, it was really very rough, and, as with many of my mother's rages, it didn't stop anywhere definite, it didn't have any specific destination in mind, the train just kept on going, knocking down women and children and innocent bystanders and sometimes whole villages and railroad stations, until at last it ran out of steam, and drew up quietly some place in the green countryside. In a way, this was the first time that either my sister or I (and I was eavesdropping) had heard my mother express herself about sex. It wasn't really a matter of prudery that had prevented it, at least not the usual sort of prudery. Neither of my parents, for example, had ever made much of a thing about wearing clothes around the house, or not wearing them. But there were just some things you didn't talk to kids about. Like money, for instance. You didn't pretend that money didn't exist. You made it damn clear that you knew that money existed, and was important. But you didn't talk to kids about it. Kids, the idea was, would find out about money their own way, and when they needed to. Sometimes, to be sure, you helped kids a little to figure things out. Hey, that's no way to use a fish knife! But most of the time you acted on the premise that kids would discover and sort things out on their own, or with their own kind at school, or at any rate with the help of masters. It wasn't a bad system, as these things went; at least it was true to the people involved, which is to say that if my mother could barely bring herself to talk about her tennis playing in public, or in front of the children, it hardly seemed expectable that she would conduct earnest informative discussions about the birds and the bees and the 137 favored Oriental positions. Nor did my father ever discuss sex with me, my sex life that is, or his, once that I can recall; there was never any doubt that these areas existed, one assumed they existed, one just didn't go on about them at the

dinner table, or anywhere else. The trouble with all
this reticence, though, was that when the wall was
finally broken, when the subject finally was broached
—the broaching itself took on a quite excessive significance. For instance, by the time I overheard my
mother telling my sister that she ought to sleep
around, which was my on-the-spot interpretation of
what she had been storming about, I was already
spending much of my time swimming in the sort of
excessively mental sexual seas that I guess many or
most adolescents find themselves roiling around in
—and the net effect on me of this overheard out-
burst was for a time to absolutely rivet my attention,
not on Leroy, or my sister, or on what boys and
girls ought to be doing, but on what it seemed to
reveal about my mother's own life. For days afterwards, all these "beaux" hung suspended before me
in a kind of wild erotic focus, even old Freddie
Chatham. I found myself looking at my mother across
the dinner table with a mixture of admiration and
suspicion, and God knows what else. One evening I
remember actually trying to steer the conversation
around to some weekend long long ago in England,
in the early twenties, when (she'd once fleetingly
mentioned) she'd gone to a ball at Oxford with some
other nameless Freddie. What was it like? I'd ask.
Where did you stay? And *then* what did you do?—
my mother looking back at me with that vaguely
amused, slightly baffled expression, and starting to

answer, and then stopping almost in mid-sentence, the vegetables being passed or something like that, stopping, shutting up, nothing more.

INTO THE MIDDLE OF ALL THIS one day appeared Henri Bonnard. Monsieur Henri Bonnard. Dear Henri. One of the most frequently mentioned, and until then most invisible, of the old beaux. My mother and Henri, I understood, had "gone to dances" together in the long ago. My mother and Henri had been on a "ski excursion" in Switzerland. My mother and my uncle and Henri had once spent a weekend shooting in Scotland. I had never seen Henri in my life, had never thought much about him, but suddenly all these remembered sentences, references, these casual one-liner reminiscences that my mother had thrown out at us over the years, started clicking together in my mind. Henri was in town. Henri was due to come for drinks one evening. "For drinks *only?*" I found myself asking my mother. "Unfortunately, yes," she said. "He's very busy. He's only here for a few days." Unfortunately . . . very busy, too busy—I looked at her for stronger signs of disappointment, but found none. As the big evening approached, I looked for deeper indications of tension, excitement, nerves, but still found very little. I observed my father closely. Surely *he* knew—I had inalterably decided by then that Henri Bonnard had been my mother's lover, and felt at the same time very grownup about the knowledge, and protective towards my father (after all, he was the one who had married her), and also vaguely angry at him for risking having this Bonnard person around her again—for not just standing up and saying, Goddamnit, madame, you had your chance with him once, for God's sakes now let him be out of our lives! Something of the sort anyway. During the first part of that week, my mother would come bustling in the door in the late afternoon, back from Bloomingdale's or the hairdresser, at least that was where she said she had been, and I would find myself regarding her as if she were some sort of exotic object, a stranger certainly. She'd be standing four feet away from me, back half turned, putting away her coat in the hall closet. I'd suddenly see her twenty years ago meeting secretly with Henri Bonnard. I would imagine them lying in bed together. An enormous villa just outside Paris. (The set from *Marienbad,* I think.) Rumpled bedclothes. Tearful farewells. Balconies. Alas-I-am-going-to-marry-another. "I thought you were making me a drink," my mother would say. And then on Thursday evening, 6:30 prompt, Monsieur Bonnard, the invisible lover, finally stepped through the doorway in the flesh. "Henri!" my mother greeted him. He kissed her hand. He acted friendly to my father, who acted friendly to him. I watched them all like a hawk. "And so this is

young Michael," said Dear-Henri-Monsieur-Bonnard,
advancing towards me. I shook his hand gravely. I
wasn't going to blow the whole thing by acting like
a kid over something that had happened twenty or
thirty years ago, especially seeing how suave and cool
everyone else seemed to be behaving about it. On
the other hand, she *was* my mother, these were my
parents—I wasn't going to let any Parisian gunslinger
come sidling through the front door and start stirring up trouble in the old homestead. We all sat
around in the library and sipped at drinks. I watched
Henri closely. In truth, he was a very good-looking
man, taller than I'd expected. Over six feet. A nice,
quite strong face. Thinning gray hair. Evidently in
his early sixties, but with the bearing and physique
of a man who once was very good at sports, and
still keeps up. I looked at my father. Well under six
feet. Decidedly frail. No longer kept up. I glanced
over at my mother. She was sitting on the far side
of the sofa, listening to Henri. She smoked a cigarette. Henri was telling a story about her friend,
Louise Ferande. He had seen her recently in Paris.
My mother laughed. My father seemed very calm.
I marveled at everyone's restraint, and vowed that
when I was older and had marvelous affairs, I too
would bring everyone together around drinks or tea
or soup and be extraordinarily calm. Now and then,
it seemed to me, Henri would look over at me,
appearing to catch my eye (not too difficult a feat

since most of the time I was staring straight at him), and would give me what in hindsight I would describe as a strange smile. I continued to stare fixedly back. I could be as goddamned sophisticated as all the rest of them, I decided, but I wasn't going to let anyone get away with anything. "How are you getting along at college?" Henri suddenly asked me. "Are you doing as well at your studies as I hear you did at school?" "It's okay," I said stiffly, and took an immense swallow of my drink, which I hadn't especially wanted to have at all just then. Henri went back to talking with my parents. He was in New York briefly "on business." He owned some perfume company, I knew, outside Paris. A fair-sized perfume company. He looked sleek and successful sitting there in his dove-gray suit. I wondered if my mother was secretly regretting not having married him, because of his perfume company. Henri said that after his business meetings he was going up into Canada "to shoot." I wanted to ask, "Shoot what?"—I was actually interested. Henri was leaning back against the sofa, laughing, the three of them now talking about some hunting expedition that he and my mother's brother had been on some while ago. In my mind I was doggedly reviewing the various Canadian animals that Henri could be likely to shoot at this time of year. "Elk," I said suddenly. They all looked at me. Henri's smile remained unchanged. "Do you like to hunt?" he asked. "The boy's never hunted a

thing in his life," my mother said. I could have killed
her right then. "No, no, I was wondering . . . thinking
about what you were going to shoot," I muttered.
"Not elk," said Henri, "although sometimes I have
shot elk . . ." I wished he would stop smiling at me.
I could suddenly see him, in that sleek gray suit,
Tyrolean hat, boots, kneeling beside some crag in
the Canadian Rockies, rifle braced, telescopic sight
in focus, pumping lead into some poor damned ant-
lered elk. Smiling. I looked over at my father. He
was sitting in the big green chair he usually sat in,
leaning a little forward. He seemed to be staring
at the carpet. All this big talk about hunting, I
knew, was finally beginning to get him down. After
all, it was bad enough having to sit around being
restrained and sophisticated while your wife's former
lover barges into your house—your wife's six-foot-
two, athletic, perfume-company-owning former lover
—without having to listen to a lot of aggressive masculine stuff about hunting and shooting into the bar-
gain. Henri turned to me, that smile again. "Sometime, if you like, I'll take you with me on one of
these expeditions," he said. "Why, *that's* a nice idea,
Henri," my mother said. To me: "I'm sure you'd find
it a very broadening experience." I looked back at
my father. Smoking a cigarette. Silent. My mother
smiling. Henri smiling. Broadening experience, indeed. "Unfortunately, I can't take you this time,"
Henri was saying. "But next year, maybe . . ." I

glared at Henri. "I don't *like* to hunt!" I said suddenly, with lunatic passion. (In fact, I had always wanted to hunt but had never had the opportunity.) "I don't *believe* in hunting! I don't think hunting makes you a better man than—than anyone else!" Silence. "Oh," said Henri finally. "Well, maybe we could do something else . . ." My father got to his feet and offered to make more drinks. Unhappily, said Henri, he had to leave. I felt very proud. My sister came in the front door. Flurry of greetings. Then goodbyes. I hovered solemnly in the background, which seemed all right with everyone else. At the last moment I walked up to Henri, shook hands with my firmest grip. "Goodbye," I said, looking him what I hoped was square in the eye. "Goodbye, Michael," he said. Then he patted me lightly on the shoulder, and smiled. And left. Afterwards, at dinner, my mother and father seemed unusually silent. My sister talked for a while about somebody called Gunther, who I gathered was to be Leroy's replacement. Gunther was currently in his last year at Trinity College, and hoped to make verse drama his career. As we all went out of the dining room, my mother paused, turned to me. "I hope you never act like that again," she said. I looked her, too, square in the eye. I felt very calm, and sure. Paul Henreid singing the Marseillaise in the Casablanca nightclub. Jackboots all around. The inner peace. A-man-must-do-what-he-has-to-do. "Okay," I said diplomatically. I could afford to lose a couple of rounds. I followed them into the library and passed the coffee cups around in a wild transport of familial solidarity.

$\mathcal{I}$N THE VERY EARLY 1950's, IN 1951 I think, when he was around fifty-five (and I was in my last year at college), something good seemed about to happen to my father. At the time, he really wasn't doing a damned thing except having lunch with people. That table at the King Cole Bar in the St. Regis. Mr. Arlen's table. He would arrive there around one o'clock, he said, although actually it was closer to 12:30, and he would leave around 2:30, he said, although actually it was usually after three. Not that it matters. He wasn't doing anything else. And it's probably unfair of me to say that he was only lunching with people; in fact he was talking with people, or to people, and he did that very well. Sometimes the people were eminences, distinguished, men who indeed were something in the world, or who had been something in the world. When he was in town in a show, Rex Harrison would come by. Or John O'Hara. Thornton Wilder. Noel Coward. The occasional presence of such people gave "the table" a certain cachet. "The table" would be mentioned in the columns, Leonard Lyons, that sort of thing. But in truth most of the men who joined my father at his lunches were of a different sort, the sleek, rather too affable, rather too easily smiling men-about-New York, men with carefully trimmed fingernails and small public-relations firms, men in charge of advertising at Condé Nast, recently arrived editors at *Time* or *Life,* pleasant men on the whole, of tepid body temperatures, who liked to stand close to something warmer. I used to drop by the table often, at first on vacations from college, then when I was working in New York, and what I mostly remember is this semicircle of perpetually tanned, relentlessly sophisticated, New York-and-I-hope-Southampton-in-the-summer faces, and my father talking, talking, being often amusing, entertaining, being often truly sharp and intelligent, and these faces ringing him around—George and Richard and John and Harry. "*Great* to see you, Michael," George would say, sliding into an empty chair. George in his beautiful gabardine suit, George who commuted to Bermuda, where his wife's family was "active" in real estate, who found the weekly plane trip useful because it allowed him to "keep up with his reading." Also, around the time I'm talking of, 1950, 1951, my father—almost in direct proportion to his own withdrawal from writing—began somehow to fasten on my own slow, amateurish, and really not very promising progress towards it. I knew even then that this was all very understandable and plausible, that no parent is capable of absolute detachment towards the accomplishments of his children. But all the same it used to trouble me that my father should seem so *very* pleased by what I was then doing, by the tiny triumphs I was then managing in the small arenas at Harvard—"the college magazine," "the college musical show." It's not that I myself was especially modest about these things. I felt an enormous glow of pride, pleasure, what-have-you, whenever I got a story into the college magazine, which wasn't in the least diminished for me by my knowledge that, on many occasions, I was the only person writing for it, and was the editor as well. I realized, too, that fathers were supposed to be pleased by their sons' achievements, or semi-achievements, and I was certainly glad that mine liked what I'd been doing, didn't disapprove, didn't ignore. But it was more than liking, father-taking-an-interest, and it began to seem out of balance and disturbing—something more, or at least different, than a son's usual embarrassment at his father's coming on too strong about his Little League fastball. I didn't even particularly admire my father's work in those days—secretly disapproved of a lot of it in fact, cloaked in my new-found serious Harvard high-literary standards to the point of being quite agreeable to sharing with Edmund Wilson, Lionel Trilling, Cyril Connolly, et al., *their* already published embarrassments at the "excesses" and "modishness" of *The Green Hat*. But at the same time, I think this is true to say, I knew damned well he was a real writer. I knew when I read some of his stories, especially some of the things in *May Fair* and *These Charming People*, that there on the page was a real presence, an energy. Somebody. There sure as hell was *something* there, something that not many other men had—I didn't know what it was, and I didn't even like most of it then, but I knew it was special. *He* was special, in a way that none of the Georges and Richards and Johns and Harrys seemed able to comprehend, or at any rate meet, with their thin laughs, and anecdotes, and endless savviness. And now he seemed no longer to comprehend it. He seemed to have let it all go by, as if it had been somebody else all along. We'd sit around that circular table at the St. Regis—he talking, conversing, conversing with himself, reminiscing. Set-pieces. The time he and Conrad and Shaw were on the *Aquitania* together. D. H. Lawrence at the Café Royale. D. H. Lawrence, Michael? Which Lawrence was that? Lawrence sketched in five sentences for the benefit of a cosmetics account executive, who kept inquiring if Noel Coward was "in town," and looking hopefully around the room. And then one year, for a couple of months in that one year, something good seemed about to happen. It was a television show, the possibility of being a sort of narrator-host on a new "dramatic" series. My mother wrote me about this while I was at college. "Your father is very excited," she said. "He and Mr. Tobin have begun work on an idea for television . . ." I remembered Mr. Tobin slightly, I remembered him in fact as being one of the Georges and Johns and Richards at the St. Regis, a tall, dark-haired, handsome, soft-faced man in his late thirties, vaguely aristocratic good looks, the sort of man who always seemed to be wearing an open-necked silk shirt and an ascot whether he was or not. He'd met my father at a party somewhere, and had started to drop by off and on at the St. Regis. He was a writer. He had written a number of unperformed plays, one gathered, "in the Freddie Lonsdale manner." He was now working on the outskirts of the new television drama programs—and he had this idea for a series. It was to be called *Knaves and Aces,* which still makes me wince as I write it (what would my old companions, Wilson, Trilling, and Connolly, think of *Knaves and Aces?*), and was to be a series of thirty-minute plays; of thirty-minute, elegant-and-sophisticated plays, which my father would introduce from a sort of mock-up of his St. Regis table.

Peter Tobin would write the plays. My father would
be the front man, the "host." Hosts were very big on
television then—Ronald Reagan on G.E. Theatre,
Alistair Cooke on Omnibus, etc. One could probably
say that *Knaves and Aces* was doomed from the
start (although God knows how one could ever be
too damned sure about anything on TV being
doomed, or not doomed, from the start). Among
other reasons, Peter Tobin, a nice man, just wasn't
much of a writer—in the sense that it's uphill enough
being Freddie Lonsdale himself, let alone writing "in
the Freddie Lonsdale manner." But they did one
show, and it ran on NBC one evening. My father
was pleased as hell about the whole thing, and that's
really what I remember. He knew that Peter Tobin
wasn't much of a writer, that the whole project was
unlikely, an outside chance. But it was as if, for a
brief period, he'd woken up, come alive. Again had
a connection out into the world. Most of the prepara-
tions for that first show took place that December of
1951. "I'm afraid I won't be at the St. Regis today,"
he'd say. "I have to be at the studio." There were
conferences with "wardrobe." Conferences with Tobin. Phone calls with John Gregory, the producer.
Tobin was trying to get ready a couple of other plays
for the series. One of them, I remember, was about
a jewel thief, and had a lot of references to polo
and to an elderly female character whose name was

Mrs. Bottomley. I remember my father shaking his head over the manuscript and trying to rewrite it. The first episode was shown in January. Everything "live," the way they did it then. My father sitting at this table, very suave, the cigarette holder, the cane, a few well-chosen words, the old storyteller himself—in fact, very pro and not bad at all. The story itself, some damn thing also about jewel thieves, a girl, and a "rich playboy." Grace Kelly, I remember, was the girl—I think this was her first part. She wore a raincoat and looked pretty. I forget who the playboy was, maybe Freddie Lonsdale. And that was it, not too bad, not good enough; and I mention it all here not because the event had some large melodramatic significance in my father's life—you know, the big comeback at the Palace, the old Writer setting his hopes on a great TV success, working his heart out, then having it all fall through. In fact, he was fairly cool about the whole business: interested, hopeful (a bit), but cool, very much the way he was about a lot of things, and I write about it here less for the events involved, whether or not the show was deserving or not, whether or not *Knaves and Aces* would have led to something, than for the recollection of a very brief time, in his mature years and in my semi-adulthood, when I saw him, so to speak, in a kind of *motion;* when I saw him connected, and connecting. "I'm afraid I won't be at the St. Regis today. I have to be at the studio."

219

THE NEXT TIME I came down from college, March of my senior year, we met once again at the St. Regis. It was fine. He looked very well. John McClain and Hugh Courtland were there. The inevitable George came by, not in a gabardine suit, but wearing dark glasses. *"Great* to see you, Michael," he said. McClain had just been down to see a Jed Harris play opening in Philadelphia. There was some talk about that. Hugh Courtland was going to Paris. My father asked me to stay on with him after lunch; he had some errands to do, he said. We walked out of the St. Regis down Fifth Avenue. A nice brisk day, sunshine. Not cold. My father now quite short beside me. A dark-blue overcoat. The cane. He had an envelope under his arm. At a street crossing, I spotted the lettering on the envelope. *Esquire.* Had he written something? I asked. In a way, not believing it was possible, believing anything possible. "Oh, it's nothing," he said briskly. "Just a thing." I let the matter drop. We walked on down the sidewalk, went into Cartier's. He had a watch to pick up. On the way out again he said, *"Esquire* is publishing a story of mine." Great, I said, or something like that. I was really very pleased, and felt quite strange. I knew that one of these days he would start again to write, and I felt both gladness and lots of other quite nameless things as well. He handed me the envelope as we walked. I took out the contents, a manuscript. At the top of the page: *The Golden Bridegroom,* by

Michael Arlen. I started to read, then stopped. "But this is one you've already done," I said. "Yes," he said. Then: "It was published in England." Then: "I've made a few changes. I think it's jolly good, if you ask me." I didn't read it then because we were walking, put it back in the envelope, returned the envelope to him. I'd already read it, I think in *The Strand,* or in some similar magazine, one of the scattering of odd-pieces he'd done before the war. We did some other errands that afternoon, I forget which, something about shirts at Sulka, a foray into Scribner's. I didn't usually go shopping with my father, in fact I didn't usually think of him going shopping. It was very nice. And then it began to get late. We were on Fifty-second Street and Fifth. "Let's drop in at '21,'" he said. We went on in, sat down at one of the small tables downstairs. Mac Kriendler, one of the owners, came by. "How come you don't drop in any more?" he asked. "Are you still on the Coast?" It was about 5:30 then, a nearly spring evening, nobody much there. My father had a Martini. I would have liked to have had a beer, but I had a Scotch-and-soda, feeling that to be more the kind of drink expected of one in such fancy surroundings. We talked about this-and-that for a while. College. Some Spaniard that my sister was threatening to marry. "I don't even believe he's a real Spaniard," my father said. The manila envelope was lying on the table in front of us. My father picked up a

corner of it, fingered it for a moment. "I was surprised at how little *dated* this is," he said. "I mean,
some of the references aren't right for today, but the
story itself holds up very well. The character of Pull-
man, for example. I think he comes off very well . . ."
He looked at me. I don't know how I must have
seemed to him. He put his hand on my arm, the way
he sometimes did. Sometimes he had the goddamned-
est deep brown eyes I've ever seen. "It would be
nice to be in print again," he said. And then very
quickly: "I heard the most astonishing thing from
Hugh . . ." The eyes quite different. Hugh. Some
story. A swirl of words. Funny. We stayed a while
more, he finished a second drink, and paid. We
walked out slowly through the room, which by now
was nearly full. Men, women. Talk. Suddenly a voice
boomed out: "Michael!" My father stopped. The
room seemed quite dark. Over in a far corner sat
Hemingway. Unmistakable. The beard. The face. I
walked on over, following my father. "Good to see
you, Michael," he said with evident feeling. He was
apparently being interviewed. "Sit down, sit down,"
Hemingway kept saying. My father demurred a bit,
the interview and all that. Hemingway appeared no
longer aware of the newspaperman. We all sat
around the small table, and Hemingway and my
father talked to each other. I guess I should remember what they said, what who said to whom, but it
wasn't like that at all. Mostly I remember a kindness

that seemed to exist between the two men, in the resonance of the voices, in the eyes, in the echoes that moved back and forth across the tablecloth. Hemingway himself had recently been having a very rough time. *Across the River and into the Trees.* Bad reviews, a bad press. He'd just been getting over a skin disease. He kept rubbing the side of his face with the flat of his hand. "Those damned doctors," he said. "All that money to fix up one's hide." Then: "I wrote the bloody book for $25,000." Then: "I don't think it's too bloody bad. I could have written five hundred pages just about Cantwell."

"Cantwell is a marvelous character," my father said. "You really did him very well, Ernest."

"They've been tearing it all to pieces," Hemingway said.

"You don't have to worry, Ernest," my father said.

Hemingway asked me briefly about what I was doing. He spoke of his son, Patrick, who was in Africa. John O'Hara. Do you see much of John? They spoke of John O'Hara. Of old friends in Paris and London. Hemingway was hoping to get out to Idaho soon. He had a cabin out near Sun Valley. There was a very real warmth across that table, and I remember Hemingway pleased, my father easeful, a kind of ease I'd rarely seen in him, none of that wit, that dapperness, that St. Regis amusingness. I don't want to make too much of what it was or wasn't. Briefly, I think, for a few moments in the dark of that room, he must have felt himself on hard ground again, known. We finally got up to leave. Lots of hand-clasping, shoulder clasping. Hemingway so big. My father small, very handsome, not leaning on his cane. "Give my love to Atalanta," Hemingway said. "I will," my father said. "She'd like to see you." Some other men came up. More newspaper people. They were calling him "Papa." "Goodbye, goodbye," Hemingway said. Then: "I still owe you a favor, Michael." A big laugh. "Goodbye, Ernest," my father said. We walked out the door, back down the street. Fifty-second Street. My father was very quiet. The cane tapping on the sidewalk. "What did Mr. Hemingway mean about the favor?" I asked. "Oh that," he said. He laughed. A nice laugh. An old private joke, he said. "One autumn in Paris I introduced Ernest to a girl I was with," he said. "Duff Twysden. Ernest later made that book around her. You know: Lady Brett." We turned on Fifth and headed north, uptown. "At some time or other everybody was in love with Duff Twysden," he said. We walked along beside each other for a while, this short dark man, the cane, the manila envelope under his arm, and then found a taxi close by the Plaza and went home.